The Random House Series in Money and Banking
EDITOR: *Harlan M. Smith* UNIVERSITY OF MINNESOTA

Elementary Monetary Theory

ELEMENTARY MONETARY THEORY

Harlan M. Smith
UNIVERSITY OF MINNESOTA

 RANDOM HOUSE *New York*

Preface

to the Random House Series
in Money and Banking

This series of books in money and banking has two primary purposes. First, it provides users of existing textbooks in the field with appropriate supplementary material in areas to which they may wish to devote additional attention. Second, in conjunction with the "core" volume (*The Essentials of Money and Banking* by Harlan M. Smith), this series makes it possible for each instructor and student in the field to put together a collection of books that will best suit his needs in terms of the amount of reading involved and the proportion of the course to be devoted to the different segments of the field. The core volume makes it possible to ensure that a basic minimum is covered in each of the areas traditionally included in money and banking courses. The "satellite" books may then be used to supplement the basic text in desired areas. The series thus provides a maximum degree of flexibility in selecting textbook materials for money and banking courses.

These books can serve other purposes as well, for each one is written in such a manner that it can be used independently, or in any desired combination, by anyone possessing an interest in its subject. The books provide, in every case, systematic expositions of their subjects, yet each is short enough to serve as supplementary text material in various courses as well as in the standard money and banking courses.

Preface

Monetary theory provides one essential element in our developing understanding of the behavior of our economy. Money and banking courses regularly include a body of analysis designated as monetary theory. The same analysis, whether explicitly labeled monetary theory or not, is needed for the study of business cycles or macroeconomics. For some time there has been no elementary monetary theory book that could be used as a textbook or as a supplement to other materials in these fields. The present volume remedies this deficiency.

The author provides here in brief compass an elementary exposition of monetary theory. The major approaches to the subject are explored systematically to see what light they can shed upon the central inquiries of the discipline and to throw into relief the unresolved problems of each approach. Thus the student is helped to see the relationship between the quantity theory of money and the Keynesian theory. Production, employment, and price level are tied together instead of leaving one or another relatively neglected as in much traditional monetary theory. The analysis is presented as simply as possible, and the student is deliberately spared the abstruse theory that is properly reserved for more advanced work. The author wishes to thank Professors William Letwin and Paul McCracken for their helpful suggestions, and he absolves them of responsibility for the final result.

Harlan M. Smith

Minneapolis, Minnesota
August, 1967

Contents

Elementary Monetary Theory

CHAPTER **1**

Introduction

Monetary theory had its origin in attempts to explain changes in the value of money. In recent years, however, some of the shortcomings of earlier theories have made it necessary to broaden the scope of the inquiry to include other macroeconomic questions. This book deals with monetary theory as defined today with attention concentrated on the following questions: What explains changes in the value of money? What are some of the principal relationships between monetary factors and critical nonmonetary factors in the economy?

In this opening chapter we must begin by making clear what is meant by a change in the value of money. Then we shall briefly consider how to measure changes in its value. The chapter will conclude with an inquiry into the main effects of changes in the value of money. It will be seen that these effects are of such nature and importance as to be of concern to most people.

HOW ARE CHANGES IN THE VALUE OF MONEY MEASURED?

Money is valuable only because it provides the holder with the ability to purchase things from which he expects to derive satisfaction. The value of any money is then precisely the amount of its purchasing power for desired goods and services. To say that the value of money has declined is to say that a given quantity of money no longer purchases as much as before or that it takes more money to purchase the same bundle of goods and services as before, or that the prices of these goods and services in general have risen. A measure of the extent to which these prices have risen, on the average, is then a measure of the extent to which the value, that is, purchasing power, of money has fallen.

Changes in price levels, and hence in the value of money, are measured by the use of index numbers. The period whose price level is to be taken as the basis for comparison is assigned an index number of one hundred. The average of prices in other periods is then compared to the average in the base period. We need not explore in detail the methods used to compute such averages, although different methods yield somewhat different results. The principal requirement is a defensible system of weighting of the various prices or items to be averaged. Commonly, the weights used are the total dollar volume of expenditures on each item in the base period. There are also practical problems in obtaining the appropriate raw data for the computations; the price quotations for each item must be representative of the prices actually being paid in each period.

What a person needs to include in constructing a price index depends upon the specific purpose he has in mind. Any price index measures changes in the purchasing power of money over the goods and services included in the index (and over those of which the included goods and services are clearly representative). So one can construct an index of the prices of food or of clothing alone. If items in the index are weighted according to the expenditures on them by some particular group of buyers, the index then measures changes in the value of the dollar when spent on those items by that particular group of buyers. The Consumer Price Index computed by the Bureau of Labor Statistics measures changes in the value of the dollar for the average urban household consumer, given his expenditure pattern. An index used to deflate national-income statistics provides a measure of changes in the purchasing power of the dollar over current output for the nation. No one index is best for all purposes. We will have occasion later to consider what index to use in various contexts.

It is sometimes desirable to get a general picture of price-level movements over a long span of time. The longer the time span, however, the less reliable the price index. Over a long period, the goods and services the dollar purchases change substantially. There is no entirely satisfactory way to handle new goods that didn't exist early in the period and yet measure change in the purchasing power of the dollar over a given bundle of goods. Indexes over long periods must, therefore, be treated as very rough measures at best.

WHAT IS THE SIGNIFICANCE OF A CHANGE IN THE VALUE OF MONEY?

The reason for extended consideration of changes in the value of money is the fact that such changes produce various economic effects that may be advantageous or disadvantageous to certain individuals or to the public in general. It is not necessarily to everyone's advantage to have the value of money increase, nor to everyone's disadvantage to have the value of money decrease, for other factors may change at the same time. The value of the dollar today is far less than it was in 1933; we all have to pay much higher prices for most of the items we buy. But a much larger fraction of the labor force has jobs today than in 1933, and those who do have jobs have substantially higher incomes than in 1933. So even though prices are higher—which is to say the value of the dollar is lower—the country in general is enjoying a higher standard of living. Of course, this does not mean that we would not be still better off if we had been able to increase employment and money income since 1933 to the same degree that we have, and at the same time prevented the price level from rising. Nor is it to say that reducing the value of the dollar is a way to increase employment and real income, that is, the volume of goods obtainable with money income. Such propositions do not follow from the contention that the decline in the value of the dollar is not itself an indication of, nor a measure of, a decline in standard of living. Similarly, we can see that the rise in the value of the dollar that took place from 1929–1933 (the price index declining from ninety-eight in September, 1929 to sixty in February, 1933; 1926 = 100) did not imply that the public was better off. It clearly was not, for we slid into our worst economic depression. So we cannot conclude directly from the direction of the change in the value of money what the amount or even the direction of the change in economic well-being may be.

There are, nonetheless, economic effects of changes in the value of money. It needs to be emphasized that these effects all derive from the fact that the value of money does not change equally in all uses at the same time. When the general level of prices changes, some prices remain relatively stable while others may increase or decrease. It is this price dispersion, accompanying a movement of the average level of prices, that produces certain economic effects. These effects may be classified under three headings: (1) effects on the level of real national income, (2) effects on the distribution of income, and (3) effects on the distribution of wealth. The effects of a change in the price level will sometimes differ according to the principal cause of the change in the price level.

1. A rise in the general price level, if not due primarily to increasing wage costs, is likely to involve a more rapid rise in the prices of finished goods than in some of the costs of production. This widening of

profit margins is likely to stimulate business, with a consequent increase in the level of production or real national income. However, the rate of price increase is important. If there is a very rapid price inflation, the effect on the level of production may be exactly the reverse. With very rapid inflation, the economic situation may be too unstable to provide a sound basis for business planning, or employees may absent themselves from work upon receiving pay in order to convert their money into goods before it depreciates too far. Such a "flight from the currency" and attempt to hoard goods as a "store of value" is likely to lead to complete collapse of the currency system, with attendant depressing effects on normal production. Therefore, while a slow rate of price-level rise may be the most favorable to business by widening profit margins and thereby stimulating production, too rapid a rise has the reverse effect. An unfavorable effect on production may also arise if the upward pressure on the price level comes from rising costs of production, for then profit margins will be squeezed instead of expanded.

2. The distribution of current income is similarly altered, since the prices of different productive services are not likely to change at the same rate of speed. For one thing, some people live on relatively fixed incomes. When there is a price inflation, these people receive about the same money income, but because of the inflation their real income is lowered. Thus people who have retired and depend upon fixed pension, social-security payments, and the like suffer from inflation more than the average individual. Some people

may be able to "outpace" the inflation; their wage rates or salary rates may rise more rapidly than the general level of prices, making them better off than the average person. In general, the most volatile of the forms of income are business profits. They tend to increase the most on the upswing, and fall the most on the downswing, of the business cycle. Upward and downward pressure on the price level generally follows the business cycle. But apart from whether people are better off or worse off in real-income terms as the price level changes, their relative position in the income scale is altered. This is due to the fact that the returns to some factors of production and to other income receivers (such as those on pensions) change more or change less than returns to some others. And how some factors are affected depends upon whether the change in the price level results primarily from changes on the demand side or on the supply side. The latter case involves relatively greater changes in some costs of production than in the prices of final goods and services, in the short run; it thus tends to squeeze rather than enlarge profit margins.

3. The distribution of wealth is also affected by changes in the price level. Here the most familiar proposition is that inflation benefits debtors and hurts creditors. The debtor gets to pay off his debt with dollars that have less purchasing power than the dollars he borrowed. This goes some distance in explaining the line-up of various groups in the history of our country for or against various inflationary policies. It has also spurred those who have savings that they can lend to search for foolproof ways of protecting their savings

against the ravages of inflation. In the nature of the case, there can be no foolproof haven to which all savers may safely and profitably flee, since the price of any asset will be quickly affected if all savers converge upon it as their hedge against inflation. The only protection against the losses inflation imposes upon savers is the prevention of inflation. When inflation does occur, those savers suffer least whose wealth is in forms that rise in price the most. Those whose wealth is in the form of fixed dollar claims upon others—bank deposits, loans, maturing bonds, and so on—have their wealth reduced in proportion to the decline in the value of money. Since the normal operation of the economy necessarily involves some fixed debts—contracts stated in terms of fixed amounts of money—changing price levels cannot change the value of the dollar equally everywhere.

We have been considering the effects of inflation. The effects of deflation are in many respects the opposite. To be sure, if the general price level declined as a result of rising productivity alone, there would not be an adverse effect on the level of employment and production. But when the price level falls as a result of a decline in the total volume of buying, profit margins tend to be squeezed and the level of employment and production tends to be reduced. A serious decline in demand for goods and services may depress the prices of finished goods more than some costs of production, thereby aggravating the resulting depression. But although wage rates may fall less than some types of income, fewer people will be employed at those wage rates, and all types of income are likely to suffer to some degree.

When we consider the debtor-creditor relationship as one inevitably affected by price-level movements, we may take further notice of the fact that there is an asymmetry between price inflation and price deflation. The absolute effects so swamp the effects on relative position that one cannot say simply that while inflation helps debtors, deflation helps creditors. A decline in the general price level increases the "burden of debt" at a time when the effects on production are also likely to be quite adverse. This is clearly the case if it proceeds so rapidly that it is not offset by rising productivity. The net effect is that the debtor may be bankrupted. So, although any dollars the creditor may be able to collect will have more purchasing power than those he lent before the price level declined, the price decline may render the debtor quite unable to pay, in which case the creditor is not really better off. Indeed he, as well as the debtor, would likely be better off either with some inflation or with stable prices. It is thus easy to see why, when substantial deflationary pressure on the price level tends to produce depression that makes all groups absolutely worse off, a mild inflationary bias creeps into policy. Though inflation also produces effects generally adjudged undesirable, more people are better off with some inflation than they would be with substantial deflation. Price stability is a norm that avoids both sets of undesirable effects, but the goal is difficult to achieve.

CHAPTER **2**

A Framework for Analysis

In the vocabulary of many people, theory is a synonym for nonsense, or at best for sheer speculative flights of fancy; what such people demand is "facts" in place of theory. And they will usually proceed to tell us that *the fact of the matter is* that the value of the dollar is determined by, say, the gold backing it has, or by something else they believe to be most important. In making any such statement, they are merely stating their own theory as to what determines the value of the dollar. It turns out that what they call a theory is an explanation that they do not accept, while "a fact" is an explanation that they believe is correct. This being the case, we have no alternative to discussing monetary theory if we wish to understand why the value of money does change.

FACT AND THEORY

At another level, the term fact denotes that which we wish to understand or explain. We can obtain empirical data on changes in the value of money, as measured by changes in price indexes. Those changes are the facts that require explanation for they are not self-explanatory. There is nothing about the graph of price-level changes that alone can tell us why the line moves up or down as it does. Anything that can be offered to explain this movement is a theory.

Some theories are easily shown to be wrong either because they are logically inconsistent within themselves, or because they are unrealistic, that is, they do not fit the facts they are intended to explain. But the only alternative to a poor theory is a better one. The world being as complex as it is, no single theory ever completely explains any single event or fact. Indeed the more adequate a theory becomes in explaining anything, the more factors it must take into account, and the more cumbersome the theory becomes. The more fully it succeeds in explaining some single event, such as a specific instance of inflation, the less the explanation fits other instances that are to some degree similar but to some degree different. To be useful a theory has to be simple. It must avoid trying to take everything into account, for this is an endless and hopeless task. But the very "defect" of incompleteness has an offsetting advantage in achieving greater generality. That is, by not explaining any one fact or event completely, it concentrates attention on the factors that operate in a variety of similar events (and omits factors that were peculiar to any one potentially unique situation). The theory thereby gains generality and extends the range of its applicability.

The problem of getting a good theory is to select those few factors that are most important and to discover the manner in which those factors operate to produce the results being explained. A poor theory may make the mistake of attributing primary importance to a factor that, while it may have something to do with the matter, is not as important as the theory supposes. Such a theory typically omits some factor that actually has greater importance. Or a poor theory fails to see correctly the manner in which some important causal factor is related to and affects the phenomenon being explained. The theory postulates mechanisms by which the factor is said to produce certain effects, but these may not be the ruling mechanisms at work.

In monetary theory, as in other fields of knowledge, various approaches have been employed from time to time to try to get a more adequate explanation of some phenomena; in this case, the changes in the value of money. We will need to examine different approaches and will find that, as in many other fields, we cannot answer all questions to our complete satisfaction nor can we prove all propositions beyond a shadow of doubt. Nor will we be able to resolve all controversies between exponents of different theories. This does *not* mean, however, that any theory is as good as any other, or that we can't learn anything, or that it won't matter what theory we hold. We can make some very serious mistakes in monetary policy and consequently produce unwanted results. A study of monetary theory can, at least, enable us to avoid some errors that might be costly. Though we do not know as much as we would like to know, we can piece together the insights from various approaches to monetary theory and thus achieve some measure of understanding of the changes in the value of money.

THE VALUE OF THE MONEY COMMODITY

There are many approaches to an understanding of the changes in the value of money. Historically, one of the oldest approaches to this was what is now called the commodity theory of money. This theory would most naturally arise wherever a system of barter gradually developed into a monetary system. If a barter system gravitates toward using certain commodities much more than others, perhaps because of their durability, divisibility, portability, and the like, this is a beginning that may lead to the development of a money system—for money is whatever is commonly accepted and used as a medium of exchange. In some monetary systems, a standardized unit of a commodity that itself has value provides the monetary unit. In such a system, the value of the money commodity in its commodity use would be the value it would have when used as a medium of exchange, or as money.

In the United States today, that which functions as a medium of exchange is not for the most part a valuable commodity at all—bank checks and paper money. Even the coins are token coins, that is, coins are deliberately given a metallic content the value of which is less than the face value of the coin. Money today is a generally accepted claim on goods, but it is useful only in what we can get for it rather than serving also as a commodity. So the attempt to explain the value of money in terms of the value of a money commodity would have only historical interest if it were not for the hangover from this type of thinking. National policies are affected by the persistent belief in commodity theories of money among people whose understanding of our subject is quite limited and who are unprepared to reanalyze old doctrines. Many believe the value of the dollar is somehow determined by the value of the gold with which it is supposed to be backed. We shall examine this view briefly.

Gold is, of course, the money commodity that has been most important in our monetary system at least since the last quarter of the nineteenth century. Gold coins and gold certificates representing gold coins were withdrawn from circulation in 1933, at which time they were only a small portion of the money supply.

The United States Treasury continues to buy gold at a fixed price, which has been $35 an ounce since 1934, and to sell it at that price to central banks and treasuries of other nations when our international balance of payments requires it. The full significance of gold internationally cannot be discussed here;[1] suffice it to say at this point that internationally a dollar is the equivalent of 1/35 of an ounce of gold and

[1] For a discussion of the matter, see Delbert Snider, *International Monetary Relations* (New York: Random House, 1966).

that the international tie to gold sometimes acts as a constraint on monetary policy. We shall examine the domestic role of gold now.

Instead of moving our gold stock around, the United States Treasury issues gold certificates to represent any gold it acquires, and it deposits the gold certificates in an account with the Federal Reserve System. There the certificates are used as a reserve behind Federal Reserve notes, our major form of paper money. Until 1964 gold certificates had to be held as a reserve behind Federal Reserve deposits also. The deposits consist chiefly of reserve accounts of the commercial banks that are members of the Federal Reserve System. Such member-bank deposits in the FRS are the principal reserves behind the public's deposits in commercial banks. At both the member bank and the Federal Reserve levels, only a fractional reserve has been involved. The legal reserve requirement for member-bank demand deposits can now be varied by the FRS between 7 and 14 percent or between 10 and 22 percent for different classes of banks. The FRS itself is required to keep a 25 percent gold certificate reserve behind its notes, and the same percentage was required prior to 1964 behind its deposits. So much for the extent to which gold has been required as a reserve behind our money. How well it serves the purpose is another matter.

In a sense gold is a strange kind of reserve, for neither banks nor domestic bank depositors can get either the gold or the gold certificates to use as money even if they want them. Indeed, it could create a disaster for the whole banking system and hence for the country if we were able to demand gold in place of our paper money or bank deposits. Such a demand could not be met by a fractional reserve if withdrawals became heavy in any crisis. As it is, the gold (and certificates representing it) are never paid out, even if there is no other available reserve. So it doesn't really work as a useful reserve. Indeed, the gold "reserve" is mere window dressing. As such it does nothing domestically, except perhaps to help assuage the fears of those who think it is needed and don't realize it can't even be used domestically.

The real question is whether the dollar would change value if its tie to gold were altered significantly. If we were to reason along commodity theory lines, the following argument might be made. Gold is valuable as a commodity, independent of its use as money; the value of the dollar depends upon the value of the gold for which it exchanges or represents. From this point of view, the gold the dollar represents is basic and is more important than the precise percent of reserve required behind deposits. A change in the reserve percentage does not change the dollar equivalent of an ounce of gold or the gold equivalent of a dollar. If the gold determines the value, that is, purchasing power, of the dollar, a reduction in the amount of gold for which the dollar stands would reduce in the same proportion the value of the dollar. To devalue the dollar is to reduce its gold equivalence, and according to this theory this should raise the domestic price level proportionately. The devaluation of the dollar in 1933 provided a good test of this theory. The price of gold was raised over a short period from $20.67 an ounce to

$35 an ounce, thus substantially reducing the amount of gold for which a dollar stands. The domestic price level did not increase in anything like the proportion called for to validate the commodity theory. That it increased some can be traced partly to other factors at work simultaneously and to some international effects of the devaluation. The domestic value of gold altered more than did the dollar, showing it to be a mistaken notion that the gold governed the value of the dollar. In light of this experience, it is impossible to take commodity theories seriously if applied to modern monetary systems such as ours.

Though the value of gold does not govern the value of the dollar, changes in the size of the nation's gold stock are one of the factors that can change the magnitude of bank reserves and the money supply of the country. So an analysis of the role of gold does not quite end with rejection of the commodity theory of money. Insofar as the gold reserve requirement serves to place an effective limit on the amount of money creation in the system, the size of the gold stock becomes important. The fact is that it has been some time since that requirement has placed an effective brake on the system, and the consequence then was of dubious desirability, to say the least. Here we are not debating the merits of tying a system to reserve requirements and gold stocks but are pointing out the increasingly limited role gold plays in affecting the value of the dollar even through effects on the quantity of dollars. The fact is that government and central bank policy now generally determine whether or not a change in the size of the monetary gold stock of the

country will be allowed an effect on the bank reserves and money supply of the country. The degree
of effect permitted is decided on the basis of what appears to be beneficial at the time. In any case, changes
in the gold stock are only one of the factors influencing
the money supply, and no longer a dominant factor.
So the main explanation of the value of the dollar
cannot be found in any of the roles that gold still
plays.

Gold has thus become almost irrelevant domestically, though it still plays a significant role interna-
tionally. The nation's balance of payments does have a
domestic impact, but even that impact on the value
of the dollar is not controlled solely by gold flows. So
we can't simply bring in by the back door all that
we threw out the front, and reinstate gold as deter-
miner of the domestic value of the dollar. How much
international factors affect our price level, how much
we insulate against such factors, and how various
forms of international money now enter into this is
a broader subject than we can pursue here.[2] All we
have discovered is that we can't analyze the domestic
value of the dollar in a framework that treats the
dollar as a mere reflection of gold, and the gold as
a money commodity whose value as a commodity is
prior to and independent of its use as money. We may
now pursue our query in a different framework. We
will look at money not as a commodity (or as representing one) independent of its use as money, but as
just money and nothing else. What determines the
value of money as money alone, that is, just as a

---

[2] These matters are developed further in Snider, *op. cit.*

medium of exchange? What we can learn in this framework is a necessary foundation for any inquiry into the impact of international factors.

THE DETERMINATION OF THE SUPPLY OF MONEY

When the economist explains the value of anything, it is not unusual for him to begin by talking about demand and supply. Can we adopt this approach in explaining changes in the value of money? Let us see whether we can.

We shall have to clarify the meaning of the terms *demand* and *supply of money*. We shall have to explore their interrelation. We shall have to go behind supply and demand, so as not to stop with superficialities, and see why these change, in addition to exploring the consequences of such changes. We begin with the analysis of the supply of money. Later the demand for money will receive our attention.

Money, as a medium of exchange, consists of currency and demand deposits, that is, deposits subject to payment through the use of bank checks. Table 2.1 illustrates the amounts of money in the principal forms for a recent date for the United States. There are times when the economist wishes to add time deposits to the total, since people may include those when they think of their holdings of money, and may behave almost the same as though the funds were in their checking accounts. However, we will employ the narrower definition of money in this book except when the broader measure is explicitly indicated. Our reasoning is that time deposits, such as savings accounts, are

Table 2.1 Principal Components of U.S. Money Supply
(millions of dollars)

	1965	1966
Coins*	3,856	4,380
Standard silver dollars	482	482
Fractional coin	3,374	3,898
Silver Certificates*	698	564
Federal Reserve Notes*	35,793	37,775
Demand Deposits†	128,800	133,300

* Outside Treasury and Federal Reserve Banks. Includes any paper currency and coin held by banks. Figures are for October 31 each year. *Federal Reserve Bulletin*, December, 1966, p. 1791.
† Other than interbank and United States government, less cash items in process of collection. *Federal Reserve Bulletin*, December, 1966. Figures are for November 24, 1965 and November 30, 1966.

not, in that form, a generally acceptable medium of exchange; for such use the funds involved need to be in the form of demand deposits, or currency.

The volume of currency, "pocketbook money," is adjusted passively to the requirements of the public. When the public desires to keep more of its money in its pocketbooks, people draw checks upon their bank accounts and are given the currency by the banks. If the banks run short of currency, they likewise draw upon their deposit accounts at the Federal Reserve Banks. And if the Federal Reserve Banks run short of paper currency, they issue more of it to meet the need. The reserve and collateral the FRS is required to keep behind its note issue does not normally prevent its issuing more to meet the need. A need for more coins is met by the United States mints, and the coins are deposited by the United States Treasury to its own account in the FRS. This supplies the FRS with enough coin to meet calls from banks, and, indirectly, calls from the public. In general, the demand for pocketbook money grows as demand deposits grow.

What is important in a changing money supply is, therefore, the change in the volume of demand deposits. The volume of demand deposits is altered by changes in the total volume of loans and investments made by the commercial banking system. When a bank makes a loan it typically gives the borrower the proceeds in the form of a demand deposit. This deposit is new money that it has created; the bank cannot simply "transfer" the money from some other depositor's account to that of the borrower, for it is not allowed to reduce the deposits of other depositors. To be sure, banks are not allowed to create an unlimited volume of new money. They are required to keep a reserve equal to a fraction of their deposits. For example, banks that are members of the FRS are required to keep a reserve somewhere between 7 and 14 or between 10 and 22 percent of their demand deposits, depending on the classification of the bank. The exact minimum figure within these ranges is set from time to time by the FRS. So, for any given volume of reserves in their possession, there is an upper limit to the volume of deposits that the banking system can create "on top of those reserves." Some of the deposits are created by bank-lending operations, as just indicated. Others are created by "investment" operations, which means, in this context, the purchase of securities by the banks. When they purchase securities they write checks upon themselves, which checks are normally deposited in their banks by the sellers of the securities. The banks grant them new deposits as the means of paying for securities. So bank deposits are created by security purchases just as by loans. The money supply, in the form of demand deposits, is reduced by any reduction in the total outstanding loans and investments of the banking system. But when loans from banks are paid off by the borrowers there is no necessity for the total to fall; the banks may merely replace repaid loans with new loans if they so desire.

While there is a maximum volume of deposits that banks may create with any given volume of reserves, the actual volume of deposits at any given time need not be the maximum possible. The bankers may keep a higher ratio of reserves to deposits than is required; that is, they may keep some excess reserves. Bankers' views of business conditions and prospects govern this. They will cut down on their loans if they do not think there are enough sound loan applications. And they will invest less funds than otherwise in securities if they expect the security prices to be heading downwards. Furthermore, in some circumstances, the banks may fear heavier than normal withdrawals; and to prepare to meet these, they may wish to keep extra reserves on hand. The amount of demand deposits that the banking system creates with any given reserve base is therefore, in part, a matter of the level at which the reserve requirement is set and in part a matter of how many excess reserves the banks may choose to keep.

What, then, governs the volume of reserves in the banking system on which deposits can be built? It is not primarily, as may be supposed, the amount of pocketbook money that people choose to deposit and leave in the banks. The amount of such money issued, less what is still "in pockets," is not nearly enough to account for total reserves of the banking system. To be sure, part of the banking system's reserves are in the form of coin and paper money, but the largest part is in the form of deposits owned by banks and held in the Federal Reserve Banks. So we need to look for the principal factors that contribute to the creation of such deposits.

There are three sources of reserves: additions to United States Treasury currency issue, to the monetary gold stock of the nation, and to the amount of credit that the Federal Reserve has extended. It is the last of these that is most important now. This is true for the short-run changes in reserve positions of the banks. It is also the most important factor in providing the growth in the reserve base that is needed in order to expand the money supply over the long run with the growth in the level of production in the economy. It is through open-market operations that the Federal Reserve exerts its principal control over bank reserves, bank lending power, and hence the money supply. Changes in other sources of reserves and in various uses of reserves are offset or augmented by the FRS as a matter of policy.

The upshot of an examination of the determinants of the money supply is that we can treat the money supply as a "policy variable." Monetary authorities may not always succeed in making the money supply hit precisely the target they desire, but in the final analysis they have enough control, if they choose to exercise it, to vary the money supply in accordance with their decisions. This is true of any system where there is an effective central bank controlling the sort of modern monetary and banking system we possess. Where this is not the case, it is necessary to make a separate analysis of the determinants of the money supply. Our own history, prior to the establishment of the Federal Reserve, is a case in point.

To tie this discussion of policy to things said earlier, we may voice a question: What provides the incentive for expanding the money supply, granted that it is a matter of policy as to how much the money supply should be allowed to expand? This leads us to consider the outlets for bank credit, the bankers' outlook, and the demand for loans from banks. On the demand side, the borrowers are primarily investors; they seek to spend more than their current resources make possible, whether they be households or business firms. Those who borrow from banks, and pay interest to banks on the loans, typically make investments that they expect to be worth the cost in some sense. If bankers, who decide whether to supply the loans or not, think the general outlook is good and are impressed by the soundness of the specific loan applications, they grant most loans. Thus additional investments are financed, and it is this lending operation that expands the money supply.

As long as the pressures to expand or contract the money supply are subject to some controls, we cannot expect the money supply to vary autonomously or in terms of any simple dependent relationship to any other variable; that is, not unless the policymakers themselves govern their policy in such a manner that there is some functional relation between the money supply and some other variable. It is conceivable, for example, that monetary authorities might control the money supply in such a way that it would vary in exact proportion to real national income; or they might alter their rate of increase in the money supply so that rate varied in a specifiable way with changes in some interest rate. If some such rule were followed, the money supply could and should be treated as a function of the variable concerned. As it is, there seems to be no such functional relation between the money supply and some other variable used by authorities to control the money supply. Policy guides appear not to be that simple. Accordingly, our analysis may appropriately treat the money supply as fixed at any one time, and changed autonomously by monetary authorities from time to time. For the most part, then, we will not here delve further into the factors behind changes in the money supply, which will be taken as a quantity and not as a functional relation (or supply curve).

MONETARY SUPPLY AND DEMAND

It has long been realized that changes in the money supply make a difference in the economic situation. Most of the analyses of the effects of changes in the quantity of money have not paid much attention to whether the effects differed if the causes of the change in money supply differed. This will be considered somewhat later. Now we will lay the background for a consideration of the general approach to monetary theory that seeks to develop a simple relation between changes in the money supply and the value of money. This is the quantity approach, or quantity theory.

In its simplest forms, the quantity theory pays no attention to factors other than the money supply, and explains changes in the value of money as due simply to changes in the quantity of money. This seems to ignore the potential or necessary relevance of the demand for money, and other seemingly relevant economic variables. A satisfactory approach could not simply ignore everything but the money supply; consequently, the simplest forms of the quantity theory had to give way. The quantity theory had to be developed so as to take cognizance of other factors. Much of the discussion came to run in terms of one or another form of what is called the "equation of exchange." Its most popular form is attributable to the American economist Irving Fisher, and is sometimes called the Fisherine or transactions equation.

$$MV = PT$$

M is the money supply, already defined.
V is the velocity of circulation of money.
T is the number of money transactions involving prices.
P is the average price of the money transactions.

The price level referred to here is the broadest possible price index, including all types of money transactions where something is bought at a price. In using the equation, the base period of the index is taken to be unity; that is, P in the equation is the number "one"; T is then the quantity of goods and services bought, quantity being measured in units of a dollar's worth in the base period. The velocity of money is the number of times each dollar, on the average, is spent during some defined period to effect the money transactions for that period represented in T.

This equation itself does not tell us anything about the real world. It is sometimes said to be "truistic." It says that the money value of the money transactions equals the money value of the money transactions. For on the left, if we multiply the amount of money spent in transactions by the average number of times each dollar is spent, we obtain the money value of the transactions. And when we multiply the volume of transactions for money by the average price of those money transactions, we also get the money value of the transactions. There are not two different things here that can be equal or unequal to each other, or equal in equilibrium: There is only one thing referred to, namely the money value of the money transactions, though this can be decomposed in two ways, as just indicated. So we do not need to worry about whether our equation is true or when it is true; and looking for empirical data to test its validity would be a fool's quest. If figures found for the variables were fitted into the equation and an inequality resulted, it would prove only that the statistics were not accurate, or at least not accurate measures of the variables that were supposed to be measured.

But to say that the equation is not a statement about the world, subject as such to empirical test, is not to say that the equation is useless. Indeed, it has been the "clothes rack" on which much discussion on the quantity theory of money has been hung. Various statements about the role of the money supply have been related to it. And other forms of the equation of exchange have been used to organize discussions that centered on the demand for money. This will be spelled out in some detail in the next chapter.

When we speak of the demand for money we are not talking about people's desires for income. There may be a virtually unlimited desire for income, since no matter what people have they generate desires for something else, as long as they are not dead. But we are not all misers with insatiable demands for stocks of gold or any other money, just to have and hold. We want money only to exchange it for other things at some future time. How much of our income or our wealth we want to hold at any one time in the form of money, to be used to get things at some future time, may depend upon many things. And whatever this amount of money may be at any one time, this is the quantity of money demanded, and it is not infinite since our income and our wealth are limited.

The term "demand" in ordinary demand and supply analysis is sometimes used to refer to a specific quantity, and sometimes is used to refer to a whole set of price-quantity relationships (as represented by a demand schedule and demand curve). So in monetary theory we may think of a demand for a specific quantity of money; or we may think of the whole set of conditions that makes the quantity of money demanded vary systematically with the variation of some other economic factor (such as a price of money, i.e., price of borrowing money, namely, the rate of interest). We will look later at what sort of demand curve for money may help us analyze changes in the value of money.

We shall see that the quantity approach, while yielding some insights into the changes in the value of money, also has certain shortcomings. This will lead us into more recent approaches, especially those stemming from the work of John Maynard Keynes and modern macroeconomic theory. We shall find it necessary to analyze factors determining real income and interest rates in order to get very far in explaining price-level (value of money) behavior.

CHAPTER **3**

The Quantity Theory of Money

We saw in Chapter 2 that the equation of exchange did not itself tell us anything about the world but did provide a framework for discussion of monetary theory. One approach to monetary theory is the quantity approach, or quantity theory. The term applies not to one proposition but to an approach to the subject, an approach that is quite old and that over the years has embraced somewhat different formulations. Because these formulations have a fairly close kinship with one another, we lump them all together as quantity-theory formulations. Differing as they do, what do they have in common? And in what respects do they go beyond and differ from the equation of exchange?

When we refer to the quantity approach, or the quantity theory, we refer to attempts to explain the changes in the value of money by stressing propositions that do two things: (1) they assert a causal relationship running from the quantity of money (M) to the price level (P) in the equation of exchange; and (2) they assert or at least imply that this relationship is quite important in understanding actual variations in the price level.

STRONG AND WEAK FORMULATIONS OF THE QUANTITY THEORY

The strongest formulation of the quantity theory proposition would be, "Changes in the price level are due solely to changes in the quantity of money." A very weak formulation is the following: "Changes in the money supply eventually have a significant effect on the price level." In the latter statement, the causal relation is long run but not necessarily short run, the strength of the effect is not quantified beyond saying it is too important to neglect completely, and there is room for other causal factors to play a major role. While there is disagreement about the merits of the approach, some of the differences are due to the fact that people are referring to different formulations. Probably no economist would today agree with the quantity-theory proposition given above as the strongest formulation; and probably none would argue that the effects of changes in the money supply are negligible. The problem is to formulate the relationship between the quantity of money and other factors, including the price level, carefully enough that it will have substantial application, and yet not so weakly that it tells us very little.

Historical changes in the nature of our monetary

system, however, have led to complications. For example, the growth of checking facilities and the demise of the old gold standard brought about a situation in which one earlier formulation of the quantity theory became inapplicable, namely that which tried to relate changes in the quantity of "standard money" in circulation to the price level. Whatever may have been the merits of such a formulation at one time, it clearly has no merit now, since gold money is no longer in circulation. We will examine shortly the implications of a common and yet simple formulation of the quantity theory, but first we must return briefly to the quantity equation and introduce into it some flexibility.

REDEFINING THE QUANTITY EQUATION

It is apparent from what has already been said that there are times when the things counted as constituting the money supply are not those of the usual concept or definition of money used in this book. Some quantity theorists spoke in terms of the quantity of standard money when on the gold standard; and, as we indicated earlier, some wish to include time deposits in the money supply. In either case, the M in the equation of exchange is, in effect, redefined. Similarly we saw in Chapter 2 that when we talk of changes in the price level we may have in mind changes in the average prices of one bundle of goods and services or of another bundle, differently composed. This implies that different people may have different price indexes in mind when they write the equation of exchange. Anyone may compare the relation between the money supply and the price level as measured by different indexes. So the P in the equation has different possible definitions. What about the V and the T? More worrisome is the question of what happens to the validity of the equation of exchange itself, if we can redefine the meanings of the variables as just indicated. Don't we have to be careful of the relation of these variables to one another if we start to redefine them? Of course we do, but if we are careful, the truistic character of the equation is preserved; if we don't define variables to preserve it, the equation becomes invalid.

The only variable in the equation that can be defined in various ways to suit different views without altering definitions of the other variables is the M—the total money supply. The other three variables must be defined in relation to one another. It is convenient to start by defining the T, though it would be just as good to start by choosing the price index about which one wanted to talk. The availability of statistical data fitting one concept or another naturally tends to influence the theorist to select concepts that fit the data. So it is not surprising that current output (real national income) may be the scope of transactions included in T at times. In this case, the P has to be the "national-income deflator," that is, the price index by which we divide changes in money national income in order to distinguish between changes in production and changes in the average price of the things produced. The V must be redefined to match; in this case it becomes the number of times each dollar, on the average, is spent for current output. What is included as money by the analyst is independent of these considerations. The equation redefined as a national income equation, instead of as an equation including all money and price transactions, clearly omits all transactions in previously produced goods (e.g., it excludes the second-hand car market, and the resale of old houses) and all security transactions (the P would not include the behavior of stock market prices). Since it is useful to know whether quantity-theory propositions can be related to the price level applicable to current production, the variables in the equation might, at times, be defined in this way. Indeed, the lack of equally good statistics for P and T when all money and price transactions are included does, in effect, preclude using broader definitions for careful checks upon the quantity theory.

One could also start by deciding to use the consumer price index, since this is the one watched most closely by everyone, or the wholesale price index, because it is more sensitive and often leads to changes in other indexes. If P is the consumer price index, then T must be defined as the volume of transactions whose price changes have been represented by the consumer price index. And V must be defined as the number of times each dollar, on the average, is spent in the transactions included in T. By thus adjusting V, P, and T to one another, the validity of the quantity equation is maintained. Statistical data used with the equation must be selected or adjusted to match as well.

TESTING THE QUANTITY THEORY

We have seen that the quantity theory is more than the quantity equation—that the latter is truistic, while the former involves propositions about the real world. As such, any quantity theory proposition is subject to empirical testing. To be sure, it may not always be possible to structure our theories to fit the available empirical data. In any case, what we need to consider is what constitutes a proof and what constitutes a disproof of a theory.

For this purpose, let us consider a common and simple formulation of the quantity theory that is potentially quite useful if true. The proposition we want to test is the following: A *change in the quantity of money causes the price level to change in the same direction and by the same proportion.* The quantity theorist asserting this ordinarily implies or says that this causal relationship is quite important and may even be the most important factor in explaining changes in the price level. But we shall not concern ourselves, for the limited purpose of examining what a test shows, with the extent to which this second proposition is also true, but merely with the one assertion. Nor need we be concerned at present with which price level to consider; we can take any price index anyone wants to use. A test involves getting statistical data on changes in the money supply and changes in the selected price index and comparing their behavior.

Suppose that our investigation shows some situation in which the quantity of money doubled and the price level rose by only 50 percent. Let us write the factor by which a variable increased under that variable in the quantity equation as follows:

$$MV = P \ T$$
$$2 \qquad 1\tfrac{1}{2}$$

What can we conclude from the test so far? Can we conclude that the quantity theory, as we stated it, did not hold in this instance, and hence the quantity-theory proposition is disproven, at least as a universal proposition? It would seem so on the face of it. But we are not yet entitled to draw this conclusion.

The proposition in question was a statement about the effect of a change in M on P. It did not assert or imply that nothing else could affect the price level. Perhaps something else partially offset the effect on P of the doubling of M. If so, is this not entirely consistent with the quantity theory as stated? To be sure it is, and we do not know, from the limited data given, whether or not the effect of the doubling of M was a doubling of P, which effect could have been clouded by other factors depressing P.

When the economist is cautious, he often adds to his statements of causal relations the Latin terms *caeteris paribus*, meaning other things remaining the same. And these are generally to be understood as implied even when not made explicit. But the interpretation of such a qualification in the case at hand sometimes gives rise to some confusion. Students will sometimes make the qualification for the case above quite explicit by rewording the quantity theory as follows: Doubling M causes P to double, assuming V and

T remain constant. And then they point out that in the instance at hand either V or T didn't remain constant, so the quantity theory didn't apply to the situation. But now we are in double trouble. To begin with, if the quantity-theory proposition is restated to include the constancy of V and T, one is right back to the truistic equation itself rather than making a statement about the real world. The arithmetic of the matter should be plain: if V and T do not change, then, merely for the equation to hold, P would have to double if M doubles. But we have already indicated that the quantity theory purports to assert more than the equation of exchange alone, so this is not a proper interpretation of the qualification placed by *caeteris paribus* on the quantity-theory proposition.

This may be the place to digress for a moment, for what our illustration of a test shows is that another common student contention here is erroneous. It is not uncommon for students to assert that V and T cannot be independent. If they cannot be, and must move together, then the quantity theory can never be wrong because it is impossible for M and P to move other than in the same proportion, even in the face of changes in V and T. It is said that every time a dollar is paid it is for a dollar's worth of some transaction (which to be sure it is, in the base period used for comparison, when P is arbitrarily said to be unity); and each change in V or T is alleged to entail the same change in the other. But clearly if this were so, it would be impossible to find empirical evidence of the ratio of V to T changing, and indeed M and P would always change in the same proportion. But the illustration we have been discussing was quite realistic; it is indeed easier to find instances in which M and P change in different proportions than it is to find situations in which they change in the same proportion. The fact that M and P do not always change in the same proportion implies that the ratio of V to T does in fact change.

What does it signify for the quantity theory that V and T do in fact change, and even the ratio between them changes? Does the phrase, "other things remaining the same," applied to our quantity-theory proposition, mean that the quantity theory really applies only if or when the world stands still, including V and T? Since the phrase is, or should be, added to most economic theories, this would render them quite irrelevant to the real world, in which change is the chief characteristic. But the theories are intended precisely to explain that world and to be applicable to it. How, then, shall we interpret the Latin phrase *caeteris paribus* and apply it to the case in hand? If we can answer this, we can escape from the second half of the double trouble referred to a few paragraphs back, namely that the theory is rendered inapplicable where change occurs.

The answer to the above problems lies in viewing the theory as an abstraction from certain types of changes in the world, and not as an assertion that the causal force works only if the world stands still. Various forces besides the change in M may be at work on P at any time, but the quantity theory abstracts from them, that is, ignores them, to make a statement about the effect of one force, in and of itself.

To say that the effect of doubling M is to double P is not the same as saying that anytime M doubles, P will double, whatever other forces may be operating on it. Nor is it equivalent to saying that if we double M next year, P will double. The last statement is a prediction of what will happen, given one action, and does indeed rest upon two other propositions: (1) that the effect of doubling M is to double P, and (2) that if we double M next year, there will be no other economic changes that will be capable of having any net effect upon P. Predictions rest both upon statements about the effects of various causal forces and upon statements about what various causal forces will come into play at some specified time. Quantity theory propositions, such as the one we are discussing, are statements about the effects of one causal force, a change in the money supply, without considering other causal forces. Such statements are useful for predicting, if they are correct. They do not imply or involve predictions, but predictions rest in part upon such theories of causal relations.

A finding that P increased only 50 percent when M doubled may, therefore, be quite consistent with the correctness of the quantity-theory proposition we wanted to test, though we may properly be made quite suspicious by such a finding. The real question is whether the change in the V/T ratio that obviously occurred in this case was due to other factors operating independently of the change in M, or whether, even apart from any other factors' influence, the ratio would have changed to some degree. We might say the same thing in another way. The implication of our quantity-theory proposition is not that in fact M and P will always change in the same proportion, but rather that changes in M will have no influence on the V/T ratio. Now the difficulty is that the empirical data show us only that the V/T ratio changes, but do not of themselves show to what changes in the ratio are due. And this is the beginning of our troubles in testing our quantity-theory proposition. For this leads us to a deeper examination of what went on in the period in question; and on the basis of such examination we may well spin another theory purporting to explain why the V/T ratio changed the way it did. Then that theory along with the original quantity-theory proposition will have to stand or fall together. But we cannot set up a critical experiment, as in many of the natural sciences, in which we can control enough factors to see whether the body of theory stands or falls. This is, to be sure, a rather unsatisfactory state of affairs; but it helps us understand why economic theories are not easily tested, and why conflicting theories still coexist. It may also help us avoid throwing out theories merely because they appear superficially contradicted, but that may have some merit to them. What we need to know, in any case, is what would constitute an adequate disproof of the theory. In the case at hand, it would be a showing that the change in the quantity of money did itself cause the V/T ratio to change significantly.

Before we move on, we must ask what we would be entitled to conclude if the statistical data seemed to confirm our theory and what it takes to prove the theory. It is as important to know this as to know the requirements for a disproof. Let us stay with the same quantity-theory proposition—that a change in M causes P to change in the same direction and in the same proportion. As a generalization, it would not be sufficient to support it even if we had found a situation in which M doubled and P also doubled. While we indicated earlier that a single failure suffices to disprove a universal proposition, we would not really try to prove this to be a universal proposition; for a universal proposition can never be proved empirically. We want to know how generally it is correct, whether most of the time, or very seldom. Accordingly, we need statistical data as extensive as is practical to obtain, or as extensive as the period of our interest. We may then find the correlation between changes in the quantity of money and in the price index we want to use. Let us suppose that we find a statistical correlation coefficient of 1.00. (If this really did happen, we would be entitled to be quite suspicious, but we will overlook this to consider what a valid correlation would show.) It would be very tempting to conclude from such an excellent correlation that we have proved our theory. But this would be a mistake.

Our theory stated a causal relation running from M to P, but the correlation tells us nothing about the direction of causal relations. Let us consider a moment the argument that an economist and a banker might get into. The economist might charge bankers with responsibility for all our inflation, alleging that banks expand the money supply and drive up the price level proportionately. But the banker might argue that he is innocent; he might claim he is compelled to expand credit because various forces (or whatever are his pet peeves) raise the price level and force the businessmen, to whom he lends money, to obtain more bank credit in order to carry on the same level of business. "Look," the banker might say, "I can prove it to you. Here are statistics showing that every time the price level rises, the money supply has to be increased in the same proportion. The correlation is perfect; what more proof could you ask than that!" The banker says the price-level change is the causal force, and the money supply responds. This runs the causal relation in the opposite direction from what the quantity theory does, but the high correlation is as consistent with the one theory as with the other. It would be consistent also with the possibility that some outside factor might change in such a manner as to cause M and P to change in proportion to each other.

This is not an easy matter to resolve. As before, it is not that facts are in dispute, but the explanation of the facts. We will have to delve beneath the surface to find some reason to prefer one explanation over another. We need to obtain some further clues as to whether money is the active factor or merely a passive factor, or whether it is sometimes one and sometimes the other. We need to find out, if possible, under what circumstances it is one or the other; and if we find it is sometimes passive, then what is the causal factor in price-level changes? At this point, we have no reason to rule out the changing money supply as a primary causal factor, though a high correlation alone would not prove that it is one.

We do not need to continue thinking of the quantity approach as restricted to the simple proposition we have been discussing in most of this chapter (a change in M changes P proportionately). What we really want to find out is just how important are changes in the money supply in explaining changes in the price level. As long as we concentrate our attention on whatever causal relationship may run from M to P, we are engaged in the quantity-theory approach to the subject.

THE STATISTICS ON MONEY SUPPLY AND PRICE LEVEL

By looking at the behavior of the price level in comparison with that of the money supply, perhaps we can at least see how close their relationship appears

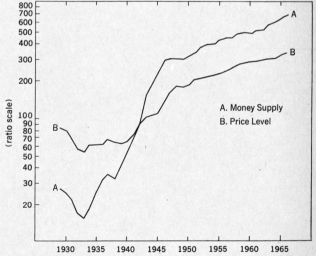

Figure 3.1. Money Supply and Price Level, 1929–1966. (Source: Table 3.1, Price Index: 1958 = 100.)

Table 3.1 Money Supply and Price Level
1929–1966

YEAR	MONEY SUPPLY* (BILLIONS OF DOLLARS)	PRICE LEVEL† (1958 = 100)
1929	26.2	50.6
1930	25.1	49.3
1931	23.5	44.8
1932	20.2	40.2
1933	19.2	39.3
1934	21.4	42.2
1935	25.2	42.6
1936	29.0	42.7
1937	30.7	44.5
1938	29.7	43.9
1939	33.4	43.2
1940	38.7	43.9
1941	45.5	47.2
1942	52.8	53.0
1943	71.9	56.8
1944	80.9	58.2
1945	94.2	59.7
1946	106.0	66.7
1947	108.6	74.6
1948	108.3	79.6
1949	107.1	79.1
1950	110.2	80.2
1951	114.7	85.6
1952	121.2	87.5
1953	124.3	88.3
1954	125.2	89.6
1955	130.6	90.9
1956	133.0	94.0
1957	133.7	97.5
1958	141.1	100.0
1959	141.9	101.6

Table 3.1 Money Supply and Price Level (*continued*)

YEAR	MONEY SUPPLY* (BILLIONS OF DOLLARS)	PRICE LEVEL† (1958 = 100)
1960	141.1	103.3
1961	145.5	104.6
1962	147.5	105.8
1963	153.1	107.2
1964	159.7	108.9
1965	167.2	110.9
1966	170.3	114.2

* Money supply, as defined in Federal Reserve statistics, consists chiefly of public holdings of currency and demand deposits (the latter reduced by cash items in process of collection).

† The price index given is the implicit price deflator for the GNP.

SOURCES: *The National Income and Product Accounts of the United States, 1929–1965, Statistical Tables;* A Supplement to the Survey of Current Business; U.S. Department of Commerce, Office of Business Economics; Washington, D.C., 1966.

Historical Statistics of the United States, Colonial Times to 1957; United States Department of Commerce, Bureau of the Census. Washington, D.C., 1960.

Federal Reserve Bulletin.

to be on the face of it. Figure 3.1 shows changes in money supply and in price levels for a selected period.

Changes in the public's holdings of currency and demand deposits might be expected to influence the prices of anything the public buys, so we should look for the effect on a very broad price index. Accordingly, Figure 3.1 plots changes in the prices of all current production of goods and services, as represented in the implicit GNP deflator used to separate price changes from output changes in national income statistics. By plotting just M and P on the same graph, we can quickly get a rough idea of whether they vary at the same rate at all, or at all closely. We know then what we have to explain, namely, why they vary at the same rate as much as they do, and what is less simple to explain, why they do not vary together more closely. Figure 3.1 is drawn on semilogarithmic graph paper to facilitate comparison of the rates of change of M and P. Equal slopes on the graph indicate equal rates of change of the variables. If one lays a ruler in a vertical direction on the page, one can see immediately for any given year on the chart whether M and P were changing at approximately equal rates or whether one was changing much more rapidly than the other. It appears that the price index line is much the steeper of the two in six years (1947, 1948, 1951, 1954, 1957, and 1960), indicating a change in the price level at a more rapid rate than the change in the money supply. During World War II, the operation of price controls served to damp the price inflation, so we may omit 1942–1945 from our comparison. That leaves eleven years in which the money supply changed much more rapidly than the price level (1935, 1936, 1939, 1940, 1941, 1952, 1955, 1958, 1961, 1963, 1964). The rates of change in the other fifteen years covered by Figure 3.1 are not so different as to be equally obvious in such a rough examination. But a closer comparison is not needed for our purpose. Nor is it necessary to examine other periods, which, to be sure, might yield somewhat different results. We shall not try to explain relative rates of change of M and P in each of the above years individually, nor to generalize about the historical frequency with which either factor changes more rapidly than the other. Suffice it to have shown with Figure 3.1 that the year-to-year rates of change of M and P are often not the same in recent years; we will subsequently look for some possible general explanations of this fact. What Figure 3.1 makes even more obvious, however, than the year-to-year disparities in rates of change is the general tendency over a longer period, such as that from 1948–1966, for the two lines to move in roughly parallel fashion. The economist has generalized from such comparisons that the long-run relationship between the money supply and the price level seems to be closer than the short-run relationship.

It is apparent, then, that there is a positive relationship between changes in the quantity of money and changes in the price level of current output, although the relationship is not always a very close one. It remains to be seen what makes the two fluctuate together to the extent that they do, and why the relationship is not a closer one.

CHAPTER **4**

The Behavior of V and T

In considering tests of the quantity theory, we became aware of the fact that when P does not change in proportion to M it means that there has been some change in the ratio of V and T. The reasons for the change in this ratio need to be investigated. The ratio will of course vary if either variable changes while the other remains constant, or if both change by differing amounts. We will look at the change in each of these variables separately, and then consider what factors are responsible for their changing as they do.

MEASURING V AND T

The availability or unavailability of statistical data unfortunately affects what we can do. We do not have statistical measures of all money-price transactions, so however interested we may be in discussing this broad a concept, we cannot actually quantify it. We do have reasonably good statistics on GNP. By correcting for price changes, we get a measure of real income (production). This is the T for Figure 4.1.

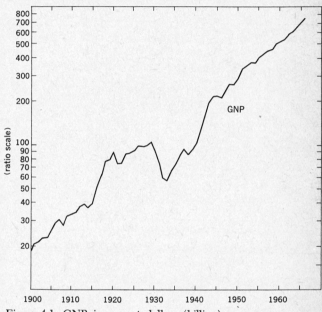

Figure 4.1. GNP in current dollars (billion).

Measuring V is even more difficult. There are data on the rate of turnover of bank deposits, but not on the rate of turnover of currency. Thus there is no independent measure of the absolute magnitude of V. The measures usually used do not purport to measure its absolute magnitude accurately, but are treated as providing indexes of change in V. It is assumed that although the velocity of currency and demand deposits may not be the same, a change in the latter will be shared by the former. The velocity of deposits is measured by dividing total bank debits (i.e., checks drawn against demand deposits) during some period by the average level of demand deposits during the period. It is assumed that the velocity of the total money supply changes to the same degree as does this quotient. To be sure, this measure is not fitted nicely to the T in the equation of exchange, especially when this is defined as real income. Many of the bank debits arise out of transactions between business firms, which are not the final purchases of goods but are steps in the processing of the goods and hence are netted out in the national-income statistics so as to avoid double counting. This is to say again that our V measure is not a good measure of the absolute magnitude of the V concept we want to use, and we can only hope that it is a reasonable index of the degree of change in the appropriate V from time to time.

There are many other types of transactions included in bank debits that we prefer to exclude, and have to exclude if we use our measure of V as a measure of its absolute magnitude rather than merely as an index of its changes; for example, checks to make cash withdrawals, checks to pay for turnover of second-hand goods, real-estate transfers, and security purchases or debt repayments. But as an index, a still narrower figure sometimes serves, namely, bank clearings. This includes only the net amounts due from one bank to another as a result of checks drawn on one bank and deposited in another. A rise in the rate of turnover of money seems likely to be reflected in a comparable rise in bank clearings as well as in bank debits. And if changes in bank clearings are then used to get an index of changes in V, we may not be far off the mark. Since we are after an income-velocity index (T being defined as real income, not total transactions), we may indeed use bank clearings outside of New York. Such a figure would exclude any flurry of bank clearings that might arise from a flurry of activity in the stock market; an index of income velocity should exclude such flurries.

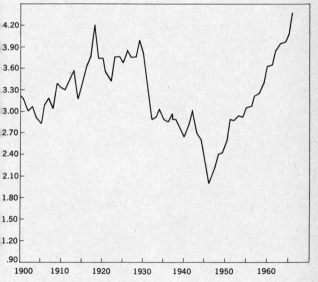

Figure 4.2. Velocity of Money. (Source: Table 4.2.)

The only other way to handle V has quite a different basis. Given measures of the other variables, one may simply compute V from the quantity equation.

Table 4.1 GNP in current dollars
(billions of dollars)

YEAR	GNP	YEAR	GNP
1900	18.7	1931	76.3
1901	20.7	1932	58.5
1902	21.6	1933	56.0
1903	22.9	1934	65.0
1904	22.9	1935	72.5
1905	25.1	1936	82.7
1906	28.7	1937	91.8
1907	30.4	1938	85.2
1908	27.7	1939	91.1
1909	32.2	1940	100.6
1910	33.4	1941	125.8
1911	34.3	1942	159.1
1912	37.3	1943	192.5
1913	39.1	1944	211.4
1914	36.4	1945	213.6
1915	38.7	1946	210.7
1916	49.8	1947	234.3
1917	59.9	1948	259.4
1918	76.2	1949	258.1
1919	78.9	1950	284.6
1920	88.9	1951	329.0
1921	74.0	1952	347.0
1922	74.0	1953	365.4
1923	86.1	1954	363.1
1924	87.6	1955	397.5
1925	91.3	1956	419.2
1926	97.7	1957	440.3
1927	96.3	1958	447.3
1928	98.2	1959	483.6
1929	104.4	1960	503.8
1930	91.1	1961	520.1

Table 4.1 GNP in Current dollars (*continued*)

YEAR	GNP	YEAR	GNP
1962	560.3	1965	681.2
1963	590.5	1966	739.5
1964	631.7		

SOURCES: For 1900–1929, John W. Kendrick, *Productivity Trends in the United States*, National Bureau of Economic Research, Princeton University Press, 1961. Table A-IIb, pp. 296–297, 1930–1957.

Historical Statistics of the U.S. Colonial Times to 1957. U.S. Department of Commerce, Bureau of the Census, Washington, D.C., 1960. 1958–1961: *Business Statistics 1965*, The Biennial Supplement to the *Survey of Current Business*.

1962–1966: *Survey of Current Business*, January, 1967.

Thus,
$$V = \frac{PT}{M}$$

This is how the data for Figure 4.2 were derived.

DETERMINANTS OF T

Remember that the T we are now talking about is current output. We would have known without looking at the statistical data that the rate of current production is not a constant, though we would not have had a very accurate notion of just how much it changes. We can look for four types of changes here, as in any time-series data: secular, cyclical, seasonal, and irregular. The secular trend of production (T) is upward, as Figure 4.2 shows. Cyclical movements around the trend have been commonplace in the past. We shall not enter here into discussion of how to measure the cycles, or how many types of cycles can be analyzed

Table 4.2 Velocity of Money (GNP/M)

YEAR	VELOCITY	YEAR	VELOCITY
1900	3.22	1934	3.04
1901	3.14	1935	2.88
1902	3.00	1936	2.85
1903	3.05	1937	2.96
1904	2.94	1938	2.87
1905	2.89	1939	2.73
1906	3.09	1940	2.60
1907	3.17	1941	2.76
1908	3.04	1942	3.01
1909	3.39	1943	2.68
1910	3.34	1944	2.61
1911	3.30	1945	2.27
1912	3.42	1946	1.99
1913	3.55	1947	2.16
1914	3.14	1948	2.39
1915	3.39	1949	2.41
1916	3.61	1950	2.58
1917	3.79	1951	2.87
1918	4.21	1952	2.86
1919	3.72	1953	2.94
1920	3.75	1954	2.90
1921	3.56	1955	3.04
1922	3.46	1956	3.08
1923	3.79	1957	3.21
1924	3.79	1958	3.23
1925	3.67	1959	3.37
1926	3.82	1960	3.60
1927	3.77	1961	3.64
1928	3.79	1962	3.83
1929	3.99	1963	3.92
1930	3.63	1964	3.96
1931	3.25	1965	4.10
1932	2.89	1966	4.37
1933	2.92		

SOURCES: GNP is derived from Table 4.1 and M is derived from Table 3.1.

in the data, or even the periods to which separate trends should be fitted. There is enough of a seasonal pattern in production that our national-income figures are frequently presented "seasonally adjusted," so we can see how well we are doing "for the season." This is less misleading than a comparison with, say, a preceding quarter of the year. Finally, there are both large and small variations in T which do not recur in any regular pattern; large ones may be due, for example, to war; small ones we typically ignore.

The quantity theory does not have to assume a false constancy in T, but the actual changes in T do at least complicate the way the quantity theory must be stated. Indeed, changes in T can lead to the adoption of a different approach in monetary theory, as we shall see later. First, we must explore briefly some of the factors behind the changes in T.

Why does T behave in the manner it does? Does it change just because of changes in M or because of other factors, and indeed what sorts of other factors? Let us first look at factors other than the money supply. The long-run growth of output is primarily due to a few fundamental factors. Output grows as the labor force grows with a growing population. Output per person is increased by the accumulation of capital equipment used in the productive process and by improvements in the techniques of production (that derive ultimately from the increase in knowledge). Seasonal variations in production derive in large measure from the inherent seasonality of agriculture, although some seasonality derives from factors that can be lumped under the general heading of customs, and from the practices of some industries regarding annual model changes and the like. The changes popularly referred to as business cycles are not so easily reducible to a few basic determinants, and theorists are still arguing the merits of various cycle theories. Suffice it to say that business cycles involve variations in the rate of real private investment, whatever the reasons for this variation may be. That is, a key feature of cycles is variation in the production of various sorts of capital goods. This is not offset by opposite changes in production of other goods, so total production, or T, varies, and with it the level of employment. We will explore the significance of this for monetary theory later.

DETERMINANTS OF V

Keep in mind that we are now talking about income velocity, or the number of times the dollar, on the average, is paid out as income in a given period of time. Again we can look at the time-series data to see whether it can be decomposed into secular, cyclical, seasonal, and irregular movements. The findings of various investigators have varied somewhat due to the use of different periods and somewhat different statistical measures. These are reviewed and analyzed in Seldon's detailed study.[1]

The data appear to indicate that there has been a slight downward secular trend in income velocity. In general, V appears to rise on the upswing and fall on

[1] Richard T. Seldon, "Monetary Velocity in the United States," in Milton Friedman, ed., *Studies in the Quantity Theory of Money* (Chicago: University of Chicago Press, 1956), pp. 179–257.

the downswing of business cycles. The seasonal pattern shows a high in the fourth quarter of the year and a low in the first quarter. The major additional movements, of irregular character, have been due to wars. War tends to raise V at first, after which there is a decline to lower than normal levels as availability of goods declines. This is followed by a gradual return to normal levels after the war. The seasonal pattern is influenced chiefly by the concentration of spending at the Christmas season. Then it is so brisk that only the flexibility of V makes it possible for the rise in spending to outpace the change in money supply.

Among the early analyses of the determinants of V, that of Irving Fisher stands out.[2] Fisher emphasized the factors that would make for stability in V, or would at most lead to an expectation of a slow secular increase in it. Habits and the stage of development of the financial system were regarded as the important determinants. Money could not be expected to move rapidly when the modes of transportation were slow, by present-day standards. Nor would it move as rapidly before payments came to be made largely by checks sent through the mails. As financial institutions slowly developed, an increased tendency to lend savings and thus put them to use, rather than holding them in cash form for the rainy day, could be expected. The system of payments in the economy was also shown to be a major factor determining velocity of money. If income payments were made frequently, the velocity of money would be expected to be higher

[2] Irving Fisher, *Purchasing Power of Money*, rev. ed. (New York: Macmillan, 1926).

than if made for longer periods. For example, if a worker were paid weekly and spent his income at an even rate until paid again, each dollar of his pay would lie idle 3 1/2 days on the average. If he were put on a monthly salary and spent it at an even rate, each dollar of his pay would lie idle one-half month on the average. It was shown also that V was affected by the degree of correspondence in timing of receipts and disbursements. If receipts are quickly disbursed (as to pay bills), V is higher than if the general practice is to defer the disbursements for some time.

All of these factors are matters of "institution" or "habit" that can be expected to change only slowly, imparting considerable short-run stability to V. The secular trend to be expected on the basis of the slow change in these is surely a rising trend, not a falling one. Obviously, although the factors just now discussed are determinants of V, others must be found both to explain the secular trend observed and to explain the short-run variability of V. Later analyses have shed some light on the matter, as we shall see.

THE CASH-BALANCE FORMULA

The quantity theory survived the early analyses of V and T because they led to the view that the major factors determining both were factors in which change took place only slowly. To be sure, there was some recognition of the effects of the business cycle on T, and this clearly required special treatment, though there was sometimes a tendency to dodge the issue on grounds that the cycle was a peculiar aberration of the system that could be ignored for the general analysis.

One of the criticisms leveled against the quantity theory was, nonetheless, strong enough to lead to modifications of the approach in a way that clearly improved the analysis and increased our understanding. It was said that the approach was too mechanical in character. The emphasis on the money supply might be warranted, but there was no analysis of the demand for money comparable to the treatment of demand in most economic analyses. For in most economic analyses, one looks at the processes by which economic decisions are made. One gets at psychological factors behind the events; and one can prescribe the elements of rational decision making in the circumstances. The quantity theory did not involve an adequate or systematic treatment along such lines. Rather, it rested on an institutionally determined V. Nobody makes up his mind what the velocity of circulation of his money should be. It is not, as we would say today, a decision variable; or it is at least not directly such. The mechanics of the system seem to translate changes in the money supply into price changes.

But surely an economic analysis should not ignore the role of demand. The demand side as well as the supply side must be important; and demand involves human decisions, attitudes, and other psychological factors. The quantity theory needed to be humanized and "economicized." And this is what some English economists, commonly referred to as the Cambridge school, proceeded to do.

To begin with, they made some changes that appear to make no difference at all. They rewrote the equation of exchange in a number of ways. Or we might say, since the symbols were changed, they wrote different equations to serve the same purpose in their thinking that the equation of exchange had previously served. We shall not bother to examine more than one of these; and we shall choose for the purpose the formulation that is least different from the Fisherine equation. Consider, then, the following Cambridge equation:

$$M = KPT$$

This, which may be called a cash-balance formula, can be related very simply to the Fisherine equation. If $K = 1/V$, the two are equivalent ways of stating the same truism.

Let us see how the new equation was used to shed further light on the subject. There is no change required in our concept of money, or of P or T, although in practice the T came to be used almost exclusively as real income rather than any broader transactions concept. M, as the total money supply, can be and was also viewed as the sum of people's cash balances (the term cash here meaning, however, not simply currency but all money). So the sum of all the money held is the total money supply. The equation then says that the total money supply is some fraction of the value of money transactions covered in T. This is still truistic. If the entire money supply turns over in income payments more than once in the period in question (usually taken as a year), which is to say if income velocity is greater than one, then the fraction K will be less than one. This is normally the case.

But the analysis did not stop there. The determinants of *K* were analyzed. The emphasis was not placed primarily on institutional factors. The size cash balance anyone has at any time may be, and doubtless is, in part, a matter of factors over which he has little or no control; but he is not completely inert and can and does have something to say about the matter also. That is, how much cash he wishes to hold is something he can decide. And his decisions have an effect on the size of his cash balance. He can act to build it up within some limits, or his actions can reduce his cash balance to zero much of the time. Now the money supply itself is not determined by whether people generally decide to spend their cash balances as quickly as possible when they come into their possession or decide, on the contrary, to keep their average cash balances as high as they can. But the velocity of circulation is most certainly affected by such decisions. If people try to hold large cash balances, on the average, they will spend money less quickly once they get it, and velocity of money will decline.

We are now talking explicitly about people's demand for money; not, as was pointed out in Chapter 1, about their desire for income, but about whether they try to hold, on the average, a small or a large fraction of the money that comes into their possession. And we see it is changes in the demand for money that alter the velocity of circulation of money. There is a place in this analysis for the institutional factors previously discussed, for these are the background for the decisions. They explain in part the amount of money people want to hold; for example, their desire to hold more when payments are relatively infrequent. Institutional factors also set some limits to how fast money can circulate at any given stage of history. But the emphasis of the Cambridge economists, starting from the new equation and the concept of demand for money, was on the manner in which various psychological factors also affect V, especially in the short run. The older approach had helped us understand the fact that V is a relatively stable variable in the long run; the newer approach helped us understand why it is a less stable variable in the short run. It overcame the mechanical character of the old quantity theory and brought the effects of economic decisions into the picture, especially the demand side of the demand-supply analysis. Let us look at these points in more detail.

We can make a distinction between the K, for any period, that is merely the quotient of M and PT for the period, and the K that represents the average fraction of their income for the period that people wish to keep on hand. Thus the average amount of money they wish to hold, their demand for money, is here treated as related in their own minds to their income, and is some fraction of that income. But this demand may or may not be equal to the total supply of money, or, more precisely, to the average money supply available to them during the period. And when there is a discrepancy, as whenever demand and supply are unequal in any market analysis, something happens—people act to change the situation, hopefully to bring it closer to what they want. Suppose they find that the cash balances they possess are generally smaller in relation to their income than they wish; they may, in such circumstances, try to reduce the rate of their spending in order to let the balances grow. The quantity theorist would conclude that the decline in spending on goods and services would result in a fall in their price level. While the money supply stays the same, the reduction in price level would bring money income down to a point where the available money supply would now be as large a fraction of their income as people wanted it to be. An equilibrium between demand and supply of money would thus be achieved.

Or suppose that we have an equilibrium between the demand and supply of money but, for some reason, the money supply is increased. The older quantity theory did not really show how this altered people's actions and thereby price levels, but the Cambridge analysis does. People find themselves with more money on hand, relative to their incomes, than they feel any need to keep—supply of money exceeds demand for it. So they spend the redundant cash on goods and services, in general. The supply of these goods and services is treated as constant, and with the increase in demand, their prices rise. Thus standard supply-and-demand analysis is used to explain the manner in which changes in money supply change the price level.

The Cambridge analysis was thus not opposed to the quantity theory, but gave it depth. It did something more, however; it opened up the possibility that changes in the price level could be brought about by changes on the demand side, as well as by changes on the supply side. From an equilibrium position, a change in the demand for money (in the desired K) could be the cause of the discrepancy between the demand and supply of money, with consequences no different from those had the initial change occurred in the money supply. Being partial to the quantity theory, the Cambridge economists did not regard their analysis as displacing changes in the money supply from its dominant role, but instead as supplementing it both by showing the mechanism's human side and by showing that demand changes can also help explain some short-run phenomena.

The demand for money was shown to be affected by changes in short-run expectations. The expectation of an increase in prices leads people to buy some things now that they planned to buy a little later; they don't try to carry as large a cash balance relative to income in such circumstances. So V is increased by an expectation of rising prices. Similarly, an expected decline in prices leads people to try to hold more than the normal amount of cash so they can buy later at lower prices; this temporarily lowers the velocity of circulation of money. Fear that income will decline or become irregular may also lead to an attempt to protect oneself by holding more cash. Desired K increases as a consequence.

So we can compare desired K to actual K and trace the effect on P when the two diverge, whether due to changing demand for or supply of money. The cash-balance equation with K defined as the demand for money (the fraction of income people wish to hold as cash balance on the average) becomes an equilibrium condition rather than a truism. The price level is said to adjust to bring the existent money supply into equilibrium with the demand for money. There is no thought here that the supply of money might adjust passively to the demand for it. Nor is there any thought that changes in the supply relative to demand, or indeed any disequilibrium between money supply and demand, might be ignored by cash holders rather than lead to action to correct the situation and thus produce an equilibrium. While the actual cash holdings at any one time might be in a sense "accidental" rather than the result of deliberate decisions, corrective action is presumed to follow.

FURTHER SHORTCOMINGS OF THE
QUANTITY THEORY

The Cambridge version of the quantity approach had its merits, as we have seen, but it inadvertently also made clearer our inability to formulate quantity propositions to cover the short run in any simple fashion. To begin with, it made apparent the fact that the short run was often characterized by disequilibrium between the demand and supply of money (between desired K and actual K). We may indeed regard the short run as the period in which changes are worked out, and within which, therefore, equilibrium conditions could not be expected to hold. Moreover, in the short run many temporary changes in the equilibrium position itself may occur. There are short-run fluctuations in the demand for money, and these prevent changes in the supply of money from bearing any close relation in the short run to the price level.

To be sure, the critical question is whether a change in the money supply itself would lead to any change in velocity (changing actual K or desired K). It appears that it may indeed lead to temporary changes, at least in actual K. There are occasional lags in the reaction that are not adequately recognized in the Cambridge analysis, and time is usually required even when the reaction does not lag. On the other hand, in some situations, an increase in the money supply may lead people to disburse extra cash at a much quicker rate than they normally turn over their cash; in this case, the increase in M causes an increase in average V. Generally speaking, we believe that any changes induced in V by changing M are likely to be temporary rather than very long-lasting or permanent. But this means that the quantity theory cannot give us propositions for the short run that are both relatively simple and accurate.

There is yet another flaw that turned out to be the most serious of all, and that led, in the end, to the development of a "revolutionary" new approach to monetary theory. That flaw is connected to the role of T (defined as real income) in the quantity theory. We have seen that the quantity approach does not explicitly handle the short-run variations in T associated with the business cycle. This further complicates the simplicity and usefulness of the theory for the short run. But it does more than that if it can be shown that the short-run changes in T are not entirely autonomous but are due in significant measure to changes in M. The demand-and-supply analysis that goes from an excess supply of money to an excess demand for goods and services rests on the assumption that the supply side of the goods and services stream doesn't change; only thus does the increase in money supply have its full effect on the price level (abstracting now from any temporary influence on K and V). But in fact, as study of business cycles shows, a change in M and in spending often does not have its full effect on the price level. If the economy is in a depression, an increase in M and spending tends to have its principal effect not on the price level, but rather on production and employment. And under some circumstances, a decrease in M and spending may, as its principal effect, reduce production and employment, rather than the price level. These changes in T resulting from changes in M are contrary to the general import of the quantity theory. It becomes impossible to state quantity-theory propositions to explain the value of money (P) without making them hinge on the short-run behavior of T (production). Worse than that, the analysis of the cycle makes it appear likely that it is the behavior of T that is most important, and that T should be the starting point for explaining the behavior of P. The quantity approach has thus come to be displaced at the center of monetary theory by what is called an income-expenditure approach, centering its attention on real income, that is, production or output. We shall examine this important approach in the next chapter and will there discover a new formulation of the role of monetary factors.

CHAPTER **5**

The Multiplier Theory of Income Generation

The need for monetary theory to pay more attention
to changing levels of production in order to understand changes in the value of money was met with the
publication in 1936 of John Maynard Keynes' *The
General Theory of Employment, Interest, and Money.*
The impact of this book has been suggested by the
term "The Keynesian Revolution"; it did not upset all
previous economics, but it did displace some of the
earlier doctrines and develop a new approach that had
a tremendous impact on economic thinking. The controversy over the "New Economics," as it came to be
called, was unnecessarily heated, due partly to the
penchant of Keynesians to be unduly critical and dog-
matic, and partly to the misplaced religious fervor with
which old dogmas and policy prescriptions were often
embraced by non-Keynesians. We shall not review the

controversy but settle for a simple presentation of the main elements of the new approach.

What is new is, first, a shift in attention from the price level to the level of real income and, second, a different set of explanatory factors. Instead of the money supply being the principal independent variable, with velocity (demand for money) the constant, in the long run, to transmit the impact of M to P, the emphasis was now on private real investment (I) as a major variable, and k (a new concept called by Keynes the "multiplier") the constant to transmit its impact to Y (now representing real income). Four new concepts were offered as underlying determinants of Y: the propensity to consume, the marginal efficiency of capital, liquidity preference, and the "real" money supply. We will explain these concepts in due course. For a time our analysis will proceed without explicit attention to the price level, though implicit will be correction of the main variables for price level changes so we can deal with "real" rather than "dollar" magnitudes of the variables.

THE CIRCULAR FLOW

As background for our exposition it will be useful to draw a diagram of the circular flow of income in the economy. This can be represented in a number of different ways. Our diagram is presented in Figure 5.1. The economy is divided initially into producing units —firms—and consuming units—households. From the households, which own all productive agents, flows a stream of productive services: the services of land,

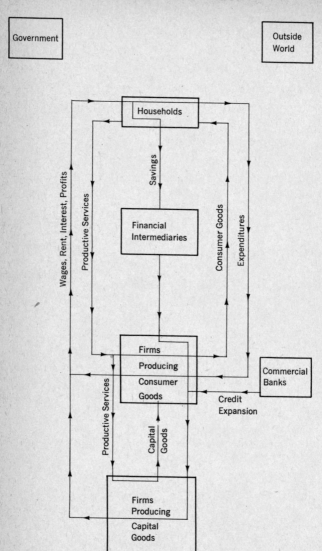

Figure 5.1. Circular Flow of Income.

labor, and capital, to use the common, simple classification. Firms, in turn, transform these inputs into finished goods and services that they sell to households. This inner circuit is a "real-income" flow, not a money flow. The outer circuit is the money flow stream. Firms pay wages, rent, interest, and profits to the households, which furnish the productive services. The arrows on the diagram show this money flow moving in the opposite direction from the flow of inputs to the firms. Households, in turn, use the money income to pay for the goods and services they purchase from business firms. The firms use the resultant sales receipts to pay out wages, rent, interest, and profits. So the circuits are complete. This is the basic circular flow diagram.

The first complication that needs to be added to the diagram is the role of saving and investment. Saving is treated as a leakage from the income stream and investment as an injection into it. To keep our diagram from being unnecessarily complicated, we have drawn all saving as though made directly by households; firms may and do save at times, and a full analysis must take this into account, but for a first approximation we ignore it here. Firms frequently do wish to invest in new capital equipment and need to borrow savings to do so. Financial intermediaries, of which there are a wide variety, serve the function of middlemen in the transference of loanable funds from savers to investors (or other borrowers). When firms borrow savings from financial intermediaries and use them to buy capital goods, the capital goods industries (represented in the circular flow diagram by F') return the funds to the money income stream by paying them out for wages, rent, interest, and profits in the production of the capital goods. The diagram shows also that part of the stream of productive services is used by capital goods industries in return for these payments; the capital goods themselves are shown to be sold to firms in the consumer-goods industries. (The division between consumer-goods firms and capital-goods producing firms is not a sharp one, but complications may safely be ignored at this point.) Commercial banks are represented separately on the diagram because they do two things that the other financial institutions do not do. They provide the mechanism for making payments by checks, and this accounts for most of the payments in the money circuit shown on the diagram. Commercial banks also increase or decrease the money supply, and hence the number of dollars flowing around the money circuit. They do this by changing the total volume of their loans or investments. If, for example, firms wish to invest more than can be financed by current savings, they may, if bankers have excess reserves that they are willing to lend, borrow additional funds from the banks. This is indeed the principal way in which our money supply increases. If the banking system reduces its total loans and investments, the money supply is reduced as borrowers write checks against their deposits to pay off debts to banks, and the banks allow the volume of their deposit liabilities to fall accordingly.

The final elements in the diagram are government (all levels lumped together here) and the outside world. We have avoided drawing the appropriate connecting lines between these two blocs and the other economic units in the diagram because the money flows and "real flows" would then become so numerous as to make the diagram difficult to follow. With a little thought, the student can figure out the real and money flows that do connect the diagram as drawn to the government and to the outside world.

There is one more distinction that must be made to prevent confusion in later discussion, and that is the distinction between "real investment" and "financial investment," or money investment. The economist refers to the production of capital goods as real investment. It is represented in the diagram by the little flow of capital goods from F' firms to F firms. This is to be distinguished from the "investment" of household savings, as for example by purchasing securities in the stock market (a financial intermediary). Similarly, an investment made by, say, a savings and loan association (if that is where the household savings were invested instead) in obligations of a firm owning an apartment building is a financial investment. Though the term investment is used in connection with the flows of savings from households to investing (borrowing) firms, we must be clear when we are referring to the money flow, as here, and when we are referring to a flow of productive capital goods.

In Figure 5.1, the price-level index may be thought of as though it were a gauge, connecting the real- and money-income flows, and registering changes in their relative rates of flow. For example, P rises if money income increases more than real income.

INEQUALITY OF SAVING AND INVESTMENT

If we look at the money income stream, it is obvious that the amount that savers wish to save might not be the same amount that others wish to borrow and invest. But the money-income stream will continue at the same size only if saving is exactly offset by investment. If the amount that leaks out of the income stream in saving exceeds the amount injected back into the stream by investors, the size of the money-income stream is diminished. Whenever it is the other way around, and more is injected into the income stream by investors than leaked out in savings, the size of the money-income stream is increased. We found that an expansion of commercial bank loans can make the latter possible. So long as a discrepancy continues, the money-income stream continues to grow or decline, as the case may be. That is, the whole outer money flow continues to grow or decline, so the change occurs on both the income side of the stream and on the expenditure side. Indeed, these two sides cannot really be separated, for it is expenditures that create income, and most expenditure is out of income, as we shall see.

Let us now focus our attention on the business firms. When there is a change in expenditures on goods and services (by households on consumer items and by firms on capital goods), it is felt by firms as a change in sales. The reaction to such changes may be more complicated than we are about to indicate, but we shall take it as a first approximation, for the sake of our analysis, that changes in sales lead, with one noted exception, to changes in production (at least if the change continues for a time). If business firms suffer a decline in sales, they cut back production. If business firms experience an increase in sales, they increase production accordingly, if they can. To be sure, if the economy is already operating at full employment, it may not be possible to increase production appreciably, and the increased demand for goods will only raise their prices. For the remainder of this chapter we will omit this last case from consideration and confine the discussion to situations where production is changed to match changes in volume of sales. We are thus abstracting from price-level changes for a time and examining the consequences of other economic changes as these would work out if the price level remained constant. Eventually we will have to return to consider further the relations between changes in production and in the price level, but our present simplifying assumption will enable us to see some things that escaped the quantity theorist with his simplifying assumption that changes in spending affected prices but not output.

To recapitulate, we have established an equilibrium condition for stability in the money-income stream, namely that the leakage from that stream in the form of saving must be exactly offset by injection of funds by investment. Note that the investment must involve its being paid out as income again, ready for respending, so the funds must be spent on capital goods. A disequilibrium between funds saved and funds invested changes money income in directions already indicated. And production (real income) adjusts to the money-income situation, remaining constant or changing to the same degree as the money-income stream in the cases we will consider.

We will want to see the amount by which the income streams change with given discrepancies between the leakage and the injection, and see what determines the height of the equilibrium level of income at any given time. We will consider the latter first.

THE INCOME EQUATION

The quantity theory ran in terms of one form or another of the equation of exchange. The Keynesian form of the income-expenditure approach uses a different equation:

$$Y = C + I$$

As a real-income equation, this says that real income (Y) consists of either consumer goods (C) or investment goods (i.e, capital goods, I). This equation may be understood either as ignoring government (dealing with just the private sector of the economy), or as including government production in either consumer goods or investment. The latter interpretation involves some problems for the analysis, so we shall proceed for a time as though government did not participate in the income stream. Our task is to explain the equilibrium level of real income, and changes from one equilibrium level to another. The short-run changes with which we shall be concerned involve changes in the level of employment, so we shall explain the behavior of the level of employment when explaining the rate of production. The analysis is derived from the work of Keynes.

THE PROPENSITY TO CONSUME

We start with an explanation of the level of consumption (and hence the level of consumer-goods production). Put simply, consumption depends upon and varies primarily with two factors: the level of our income, and what Keynes has called our "propensity to consume." The propensity refers to that whole bundle of factors that make us disposed to spend various amounts on consumption at various levels of real income. It can be represented by a curve, as in Figure 5.2, which is, in effect, a consumer demand curve, with real income as the independent variable. It is drawn here not on the basis of statistics, though it can be so drawn, but on the basis of two facts of common knowledge. First, if our real income is low enough we do not save any income but spend it all on consumption. This is represented on the diagram by the point where the consumption function crosses a forty-five degree angle line. Second, increases in real income above that level increase both our consumption and our saving. This is represented by a consumption function line with a slope less than one. Statistical evidence suggests that the extent to which consumption changes with changes in income can be represented most simply, and as a good enough approximation for many purposes, by drawing a straight-line relationship between consumption and income on this diagram.

The proposition that consumption varies in this

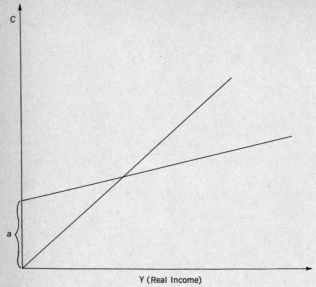

Figure 5.2. The Consumption Function.

fashion with income can be indicated in the following
equation:

$$C = a + bY$$

This says that consumption is a function of income
such that consumption is a certain constant amount
plus a fraction of income. This is a good first approximation to the explanation of the C in the income
equation.

But it will be noticed that if we replace the C in
the income equation by the above expression, we have
Y on both sides of the equation. This is unsatisfactory,
so we solve the equation for Y as follows:

$$Y = a + bY + I$$
$$Y - bY = a + I$$
$$Y(1 - b) = a + I$$
$$Y = (a + I) \frac{1}{1 - b}$$

If we know the values in the consumption function and the rate of investment, we know the equilibrium level of income. Thus, we can put in values for a, b, and I and solve for Y. The b is the slope of the consumption function; it is the ratio of increase in consumption to the increase in income that induces it. This is called the marginal propensity to consume. The a and I are, in effect, injections into the income stream and are not represented here as a function of any other variable.

Let J stand for such injections into the income stream, and k stand for $1/1 - b$, which is the amount by which J is multiplied. Then the determination of income equation can be written as follows:

$$Y = kJ$$

This is the Keynesian "multiplier theory of income." It shows the equilibrium income for a given level of injections into the income stream and a given marginal propensity to consume. It follows that equilibrium income is always some multiple of a constant rate of injections into the income stream.

THE MULTIPLIER PROCESS OVER TIME

The multiplier is a versatile tool of analysis, for it can also be used to show the movement of income over time. We shall follow an example of a discrepancy between S and I, such as was presented earlier in this chapter, and see how much income changes as a result. We will also show how the money supply may be worked into the analysis. Let us start with an equilibrium into which we introduce the following change: an increase in the rate at which capital goods are being produced and sold. This is a rise in the rate of real investment. The new higher rate is supposed to continue indefinitely, period after period. The results are shown in Figure 5.3. The base line is the previous equilibrium level of real income. Each rise in income (whether C or I) is represented by a bar of the appropriate height measured on the income axis. The constant, higher rate of investment is shown by the bottom string of blocks in the diagram. The diagram is drawn for an increase of $100 million in investment per period, and for a marginal propensity to consume of four-fifths.

The rise in income in each period induces a rise in consumption four-fifths as large in the subsequent period. Figure 5.3 illustrates how income then rises slowly to a new equilibrium $5 \times \$100$ million higher than the old level. The new income level is held constant when the rate that saving leaks out of the income stream equals the rate at which investment reinjects it into the stream. Think of income in each time period (t) being spent in the next period $(t + 1)$ and generating income again in that period $(t + 1)$, or being saved in the period $(t + 1)$ and used to finance the new investment in the period $(t + 1)$. One can then compare saving and investment in each period. For example, in

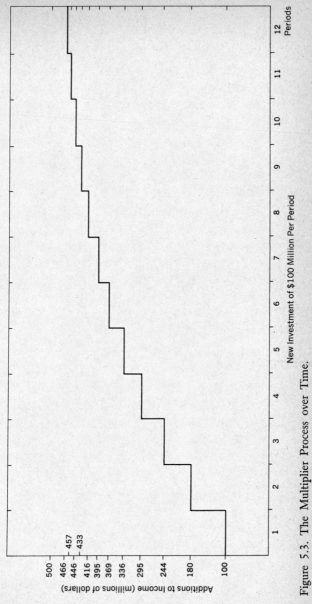

Figure 5.3. The Multiplier Process over Time.

period one, investment is $100 million higher than be-
fore, and income is raised that much. Of this, $80 mil-
lion is spent in period two, and $20 million is saved and
invested. But investment in period two is $100 million
higher than before, so investment exceeds savings by
$80 million in that period, and income in the period
is just $80 million higher than the preceding period as
a consequence.

This brings us to consideration of the money supply, for an expansion of loans by commercial banks
is the easiest way to envision the financing of that part
of the new investment that cannot be financed by
saving. A little computing will convince us that although new money creation starts by financing the
entire $100 million new investment in period one, the
amount of further money creation drops to $80 million
in period two, to $64 million in period three, and so
on. The amount of money created in each period is
lower than the preceding one (as the excess of I
over S drops) by 1/5 (the marginal propensity to
save). When saving per period rises to $100 million
more per period than in the original equilibrium, equal
to the higher rate of real investment, the money supply ceases to grow. The total growth can be computed
by summing the decreasing geometric series indicated
above; this will be found to be the same multiplier
we have discussed, (5), times the increase in M in
the first period ($100), or $500 million. This is the
amount by which income is higher per period than
initially.

In this example we have allowed for the time lags
that occur in the circular flow; it is the time required

for money to circulate, for goods production to respond, for money incomes to rise and be spent or saved and invested. The lags are many, but we have allowed for them in a very simple way—by the period analysis we have employed, with income spent or saved a period after its receipt. Actually, we have made our period cover all the lags and correspond to the length of time in which each dollar, on the average, is spent as income once. Dividing annual national income by the average money supply in the year gives the income velocity of money; dividing the length of the year by that velocity figure gives the length of period used in our analysis. Given our example in conjunction with Figure 5.3 we have some idea how rapidly the multiplier effect works.

It is worth noting that, even though we have been simplifying by omitting government and the outside world, the multiplier analysis is applicable to them also, and their existence affects the multiplier process we have described. Indeed, when we speak of leakages from the income stream, we need to list saving, taxes, and imports; while when we speak of injections into the income stream, we need to include investment, government expenditures, and exports. The multiplier can be applied to positive or negative changes in any of these injections. Any and all of the leakages actually affect the magnitude of the multiplier. They may be taken into account most simply as affecting the *b*, or marginal propensity to consume. More complicated formulas may, however, be employed when desired. The equilibrium condition is equality between leakages and injections in the aggregate. Imbalances in any pair of leakages and injections have no aggregate multiplier effect if balanced by opposite inequalities in other leakages and injections.

DETERMINANTS OF REAL INVESTMENT

So far we have explained C, but we have not explained the I in the income equation, though we have seen that much can be said about consequences of changes in I. A fully satisfactory explanation of the behavior of I has not yet been achieved, but we can set forth in simple terms the Keynesian approach to the problem.

We measure along the horizontal axis in Figure 5.4 amounts of money that might be invested in new

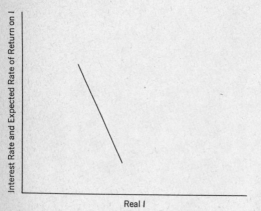

Figure 5.4. The Marginal Efficiency of Capital.

capital goods. The vertical axis measures rates of return on investment at the margin. The curve drawn shows how much investors could invest at some given time with the expectation that their investments would yield the rate of return shown on the curve (or better) for that amount of investment. The curve is downward sloping. That is, we would expect to find more opportunities for real investment to yield a return of 5 percent or better than opportunities expected to yield 15 percent or better. If someone can borrow money at some given rate of interest and invest in capital goods from which he expects to earn a higher rate of return, it is clearly profitable for him to do so. Keynes' theory asserts that as people seize such opportunities for profitable investment the rate of investment is pushed to the point where the expected rate of return and the interest rate are equal. The vertical axis in Figure 5.4 can therefore be thought of as either the expected rate of return on new capital investment or the rate of interest. The curve then shows how the rate of real investment varies with the rate of interest. This is a sort of aggregate demand curve for capital goods, with the rate of purchase and production of them a function of the price of funds to buy them (the interest rate). Behind the curve lie the multitudinous factors that affect investors' expectations of the rate of return on new capital goods. Changes in these that make investors more optimistic would be represented by moving the curve to the right in Figure 5.4, and more pessimistic by moving it to the left. As it turns out, changes in the rate of real investment can be explained better by shifts in the curve (changes in expectations) than by movements along it in response to changes in interest rates. But the state of expectations at a given time (the position of the curve at the time) is the factor that is important in the determination of the equilibrium income at the time. Keynes called this curve, and the state of mind that it represents, the marginal efficiency of capital. The term is also used at times to refer to a single expected rate of return on a piece of new capital equipment.

SUMMARY

In Chapter 4 we found it necessary to include in our analysis an investigation of the factors determining the level of income; in Chapter 5 we have found it possible to conduct such an investigation in very simple terms. Confining ourselves first to the private sector of the economy, we saw that the circular flow of income consists of two components, consumption and investment, and that the latter injects funds "leaking out of the stream" in saving. The division of income between consumption and saving is determined by the propensity to consume, which is a matter of people's desires and the level of real income. The rate of real investment is determined by the marginal efficiency of capital, which is a matter of expectations regarding the likely rate of return on new capital goods and, to a lesser degree, by the rate of interest. Changes in the rate of real investment (or other injections into the income stream) were shown to produce changes in the level of real income. The ratio between these changes (the multiplier) depends on the marginal propensity to consume. So, in the end, we are able to say not only the direction in which the income stream changes with an alteration in the balance between leakages and injections, but can say also how much income changes in such circumstances to restore the balance and reach a new equilibrium.

CHAPTER **6**

Money in the Keynesian Analysis

So far in the Keynesian analysis, money has only been mentioned to show that it might expand to help finance an increase in investment. But fuller account than this needs to be taken of the demand and supply of money. In doing so, we shall introduce another concept. We shall not talk about the number of dollars (or other currency unit) in the money supply, but about the value of the total money supply, or as we would usually say, about the "real" money supply, the number of dollars in relation to the price level. With a given dollar money supply, the real money supply would fall if the price level rose. To be sure this supposes that there are factors, other than the supply of dollars, that might cause the price level to change. The real money supply is presumed to be a policy variable that can be determined by monetary authorities, and, as before, the supply is taken as fixed at any given time and not changing in any systematic way as a function of any other variable.

THE COST OF HOLDING MONEY

The next important innovation is that Keynes called attention to the cost of holding money. The quantity theory talked about the demand for money, but unlike most demand theory it did not explicitly relate the quantity demanded to the price. Keynes did just that. He contended that the size of cash balances (money balances) that people wish to hold is a function of the cost or price paid to hold such balances. The alternative to holding cash that he considered at this point was lending the money to someone else and, of course, receiving interest on the loan in return. To hold cash instead is to forego this interest, and the foregone interest is the cost or price of remaining liquid (i.e., in possession of cash itself). People prefer being in a liquid to an illiquid position, since there are advantages to liquidity (about which more will be said later). How much liquidity they will choose to hold will normally vary inversely to the cost of being liquid. This is to say that the quantity of money people wish to hold will decrease the higher the interest rate. Remember that when we speak (in the context of the Keynesian system) of money balances, we are talking not just of the number of dollars but of the number of dollars of given purchasing power or value. It is a certain amount of purchasing power that people desire to hold in cash-balance form, and it is this that varies with the rate of interest. This can be shown in a diagram, Figure 6.1, where the amount of such cash balances people wish to hold is measured to the right along the horizontal axis. This is a demand curve for real money in the Keynesian system.

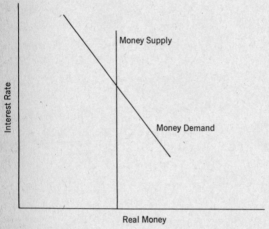

Figure 6.1. Liquidity Preference and Real Money Supply.

The supply of real money is at any one time some fixed amount, and hence may be represented on the same diagram as a vertical line. What is the significance of the intersection of the demand and supply curves for real money? It shows that rate of interest at which the quantity of real balances desired is exactly equal to the available supply of real balances in the aggregate. Should the interest rate not be at that equilibrium level, it will be brought to that level. For suppose the rate is above the equilibrium level; people will feel they should not hold such large cash balances when the interest to be earned by lending more is so high. Their reaction was somewhat simplified in the Keynesian analysis at this stage by saying that they would then invest (make a financial investment) in fixed interest-bearing bonds. This would not reduce the amount of money that people would be holding in the aggregate, though balances would be redistributed, but the increased demand for bonds would raise their price, and, since the interest paid on them is fixed, would lower their yield. This would lower the rate of interest that could be earned by lending. The reaction would continue until the effective rate of interest would again be at the equilibrium level, and cash balances would no longer be considered high at that level of interest. Similarly, if the rate of interest were below equilibrium, people would sell bonds to become more liquid and would succeed instead in lowering bond prices and thus raising effective interest rates until the existent money supply was all they desired to hold. At this stage in our analysis, then, the rate of interest is determined by the demand and supply of real money, the term "liquidity preference" being used for the demand of money. Interest is seen to be a cost of holding cash, or we might say, with Keynes, a reward for parting with liquidity. It is not a reward simply for saving, for savings might be hoarded rather than lent; it is a return on loans. By treating interest as a reward for saving, earlier economists presumed that people would not try to keep any of their savings in cash form but would indeed lend them.

MOTIVES FOR HOLDING MONEY

In the quantity theory, the demand and supply of money (dollars) determined the price level; thus far in the Keynesian analysis, the demand and supply of real money seems to determine the rate of interest. In the quantity theory, the quantity of money demanded, that is, the size of cash balances that people wanted to hold, was taken to be an increasing function of PT, defined as real income. In the Keynesian analysis, the quantity of money demanded is taken to be a decreasing function of the rate of interest on, say, bonds. Is there an error here, on the part of the one theory or the other, as to the proper independent variable in the demand function for money? As we move more deeply into the Keynesian analysis we find contributions to a classification of the motives for holding cash balances, and the two simple views that seem to conflict can be combined into a fuller understanding of the factors lying behind the demand for money.

The quantity theorist had in mind chiefly what is now termed the "transactions motive" for holding cash. Money is held because the dates at which money is received and at which it needs to be disbursed do not coincide. It is held to undertake planned expenditures in the future. The amount of money needed for these future transactions rises with the level of income, for transactions rise with income. The dollar money balances needed for normal transactions rise with the price level as well as with real income; but if we speak in terms of real money, the cash balances desired rise with real income but not with the price level.

In addition to holding some cash for the expected transactions during a period before additional cash becomes available, people may hold some cash to be able to deal with the unforeseen. Unexpected emergencies may arise in which cash is needed, and it may be very disadvantageous to be caught without some additional cash at such a time. (It must be remembered that the term "cash" in this context means money in the pocket or in the checking account, not only the former.) There is another type of unforeseeable situation for which people may hold some cash— that is, the opportunity for favorable purchases. It bothers some people a good deal if they come across unexpected bargains they cannot take advantage of because they do not have the ready money. Holding money to deal with the unforeseeable, whether favorable or unfavorable, is referred to as the precautionary motive for holding money. In general, the amount of money people tend to hold due to this motive likely increases with real income.

Other factors will, of course, affect the demand for money for this purpose. If credit is readily available, at reasonable cost, for the types of expenditure that might be called for, then, of course, people will not find the precautionary motive as strong as otherwise. And if they have many liquid assets, it will be weak similarly, for they can then get the cash when needed. An asset's liquidity is judged by the speed and ease with which it can be converted into cash without an appreciable risk of capital loss.

Keynes' principal contribution to the analysis of the motives for holding cash was the concept of the "speculative motive." This referred to the tendency to hold cash rather than to invest in bonds if the interest rate was expected to rise. It is "speculation" on a rise in the rate of interest. If, by waiting, one can invest at a higher yield, it may pay to do so, even if some interest is lost in the meantime. This may be especially true if one considers the fact that a rise in the rate of interest means a fall in the price of fixed interest-bearing bonds. For if one invested in bonds and then their price fell, one would suffer a capital loss if he needed to get his money out of the bonds again. So people who think that the rate of interest is below what they consider normal for the circumstances will tend to keep their saving in cash rather than invest it in bonds. Presumably, the lower the actual interest rate, the more people will consider the rate too low and likely to rise; and, hence, the greater the aggregate desire to hold cash, the lower the actual rate of interest. Keynes also pointed out that people may accumulate cash prior to investing it in bonds, quite apart from the expected behavior of interest, and he termed this the finance motive. So even if the interest rate was not expected to change, some cash would be held as a temporary alternative to bonds.

While these several motives combine to explain what lies behind the demand for money, they are probably not to be taken as implying that people set aside so much cash for each purpose separately, so that we simply add these amounts to get their total demand for cash. In a sense, a given balance may be partly satisfying different purposes at the same time.

What has been said now leads to the conclusion that the total demand for cash balances is such that

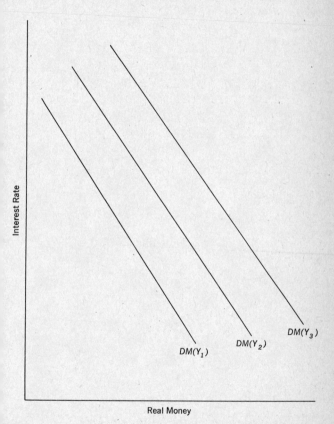

Figure 6.2. The Total Demand for Cash Balances (Real Money). (NOTE: The curves show the demand for money (DM) at successively higher levels of real income, Y_1, Y_2, and Y_3.)

the specific quantity of money demanded is a function of two independent variables: the rate of interest (as a cost of holding cash) *and* the level of real income. The liquidity-preference diagram, Figure 6.1, needs to be modified to show this. One way to do so is to label the original curve as valid for some given real-income level, and to draw a set of similar curves to the right of it representing the demand for money at successively higher real-income levels. See Figure 6.2. Alternatively, a three-dimensional figure may be used. The quantity of money demanded, given the strength at some particular time of the underlying motives for holding cash, can be shown to rise with rising real income and to fall when moving along the interest axis to higher interest rates.

EQUILIBRIUM BETWEEN THE DEMAND
AND SUPPLY OF MONEY

When the demand for money is described as just now indicated, it could be represented as a surface in a three-dimensional figure. The surface is tilted upward in the direction indicating higher real income and downward in the direction of higher interest rates. The supply of real money, fixed in amount at any given time, can be represented as another surface, a constant distance above the base plane, running through the interest and incomes axes; the distance is of course measured along the money axis in the three-dimensional figure. These two surfaces intersect in a line. That line shows all the combinations of interest rate and real income for which the quantity of money demanded (given the strength of the underlying motives) is equal to the given money supply. This line, shown in two dimensions in Figure 6.3, pictures the equilibrium conditions for equilibrium between the

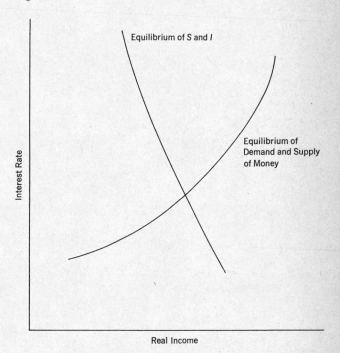

Figure 6.3. Aggregative Equilibrium. (NOTE: This diagram was initially developed, as an interpretation of the Keynesian systems, by the English economist J. R. Hicks.)

demand and supply of money. It shows, for example, that if the level of real income increases, thus increasing the quantity of money demanded, the equilibrium can be restored, given the fixed quantity of money, by a rise in the rate of interest that tends to lower again the quantity demanded. Thus the equilibrium condition is shown by a line in which interest and real income rise or fall together. Only if they do so to a degree appropriate to the underlying motives for holding money can the quantity of money demanded be kept equal to the fixed supply of money.

The equilibrium line becomes vertical at some point, namely that at which desired money balances cannot be reduced further whatever inducement higher interest rates provide. The velocity of money has then reached its maximum for the given situation, that is, until institutional or other factors change. (This implies that there is a maximum income level that can, at any given time, be supported by a given money supply, though we will not normally be at that extreme.) At the lower left end of the curve it may become horizontal, for there may be some minimum below which the interest rate cannot be pushed, due to institutional lending costs if nothing else.

AGGREGATIVE EQUILIBRIUM

In this chapter we have seen the condition for equilibrium with respect to the demand and supply of money. In the preceding chapter we saw that injections equal to leakages was a condition for equilibrium real income. It appears that there are really two equilibrium conditions for the economy that must be met at the same time. Let us explore the relation between these two conditions.

Any change in S or I changes real income, which

is an independent variable in the monetary sphere; and with a change in real income, the monetary equilibrium will be upset. If the rate of interest were to be changed in order to restore monetary equilibrium, would this have an effect on S or I? Our analysis this far has not considered the effect of the interest rate on saving. Pre-Keynesian economics (classical economics in this broadest sense of the term) always maintained that saving was affected by interest rates. Keynes showed income to be the principal determinant of saving, but there is no reason why we should not take account of some influence of the interest rate also on saving. Probably aggregate saving tends to increase with an increase in the rate of interest as the classical economists thought, though perhaps the change is not as great as they thought. In any case, real investment tends to be lowered by a rise in interest rates, as the marginal efficiency of capital diagram, Figure 5.4, showed. Maybe we should also take into account the possibility that at high levels of prosperity there are more opportunities for profitable investment than at low levels of output; that is, perhaps we should represent real investment as a rising function of real income.

If we take into account the possible relationships discussed in the preceding paragraph, we find that the same two independent variables, interest rate and real income, underlie changes in the quantities of S, I, and quantity of money demanded. Each of the last three is a function of interest and income. We have already shown how a three-dimensional representation of the monetary equilibrium is necessary. Similarly, the equilibrium income condition now needs to be represented in three dimensions, with interest and real income axes forming a base plane, and saving and investment (or in a broader analysis, all leakages and injections) measured along the third axis and above the plane. One surface represents the way that saving rises as real income rises and rises also to some degree as we move out the interest-rate axis. A different surface represents the decline in real investment as we move to higher rates of interest, and perhaps the rise in I as we move to higher income. These two surfaces intersect in a line that shows all combinations of interest rate and real income for which saving will equal investment (or leakages equal injections in the broader analysis), given the underlying propensity to consume or save and the underlying marginal efficiency of capital. The resultant equilibrium condition is shown in Figure 6.3 as a downward sloping line. An example will relate it to what we did earlier. If developments in the monetary sphere cause interest to fall, the resultant excess of investment over saving can be corrected, and a new equilibrium between S and I restored if real income rises some appropriate amount.

This sounds like the multiplier, and indeed it is, but we can shortly see it as part of the aggregate-equilibrium picture. The four basic determinants of equilibrium are the propensity to consume (from which the portion of income saved is obviously derived), the marginal efficiency of capital, the demand for money (liquidity preference in the broad sense including all motives for holding money), and the real money supply. The first two of these establish one equilibrium condition, namely that which equates S and I; the second two basic determinants establish a second equilibrium condition, namely that which equates the demand and supply of real money. The two conditions are shown in Figure 6.3 as already indicated. And clearly, the two conditions can be satisfied simultaneously by only one level of real income and one interest rate. *The four determinants thus explain the equilibrium levels of real income and of interest.*

This may be said in another way. The analysis to now has probed our attitudes and disposition to act in a number of respects and has concluded, in effect, that our "psychological disposition" or our "frame of mind" is, given the real-money supply, the ultimate determinant of the interest rate and level of real income. With a certain frame of mind or set of attitudes and a given real-money supply, only one interest rate and level of real income can result, except for a short time while the system is moving to the equilibrium values. The frame of mind, if we call it that for the present, has been analyzed as consisting of three parts. (1) We have certain attitudes toward spending our income on consumer goods and toward saving some of it; we referred to these attitudes as comprising our propensity to consume (or occasionally referred to the propensity to save, which is merely looking at this set of attitudes from the other side). These attitudes determine how much we spend or save at various income and interest levels. The attitude can change to be sure, and the consequences can then be discovered by shifting the consumption-function, or savings-function, line on a diagram, and in turn seeing the shift in the equilibrium condition. For example, a desire to save less and consume more raises the consumption function line and moves the *S-I* equilibrium line in Figure 6.3 to the right. (2) Our frame of mind includes certain expectations regarding the profitability of investment in new capital goods. Many things go into that set of expectations, and they can change from time to time for many reasons. But at any given time, our outlook can be represented by a diagram called the marginal efficiency of capital, which shows how much will be invested in new capital goods at various possible interest rates and income levels so long as that outlook itself doesn't change. When it changes, we represent that by a shift in the marginal efficiency curve and thus in the *S-I* equilibrium line. Growing pessimism among investors would be represented by a shift to the left of the marginal efficiency curve as drawn earlier and of the *S-I* line in Figure 6.2. (3) For the variety of reasons we have discussed, people prefer to be liquid rather than illiquid, but the intensity of their desire for liquidity (their demand for money) as against, say, bonds, is what determines the quantity of money they will try to hold, on the average, at various interest rates and at various levels of income. When the desire or attitude changes, we represent this by a shift in the set of liquidity-preference curves and a resultant shift of the money-equilibrium curve. For example, an increase in the underlying desire for liquidity is shown by moving liquidity-preference curves to the right and moving the money-equilibrium curve in Figure 6.3 to the left.

Changes in the equilibrium levels of income and interest are brought about by changes in one or another of these three sets of attitudes or by changes in the real money supply. We can go further, as a result of prolonged study of business cycles and economic growth, and say that the most important dynamic factor in the economy is the behavior of the marginal efficiency of capital; in other words, most important are the changes in the outlook for profitable real investment.

When marginal efficiency improves, investment rises and the multiplier process brings us to a new, higher level of income. Let us look at this now in terms of our dual-equilibrium diagram, Figure 6.3, which will be recognized as the key diagram in the analysis. The shift of the marginal efficiency of capital moves the S-I equilibrium curve to the right. If the money supply responds as we supposed in our example in Chapter 5, the money-equilibrium curve in Figure 6.3 moves to the right also; we tacitly assumed it to move far enough that the rise in real income via the multiplier process would not entail any rise in the equilibrium rate of interest. If, however, the money supply is not permitted to rise, or for any reason does not rise, the increased investment will have to be financed by tapping temporarily idle money. To induce the lending of this money will require a higher rate of interest to overcome people's liquidity preference sufficiently. This is seen in Figure 6.3; when the money-equilibrium curve remains constant and the S-I curve moves right, interest rates are increased. Note also that in this case the equilibrium level of income does not rise by quite as much as in the earlier multiplier example. The multiplier analysis thus gives but an approximate estimate of the change in equilibrium income; the actual outcome depends partly on the behavior of the money supply. One could say this differently by saying that the behavior of the money supply has some effect on the magnitude of the real multiplier.

SUMMARY

We have discovered in Chapter 6 that money cannot be omitted from the determination of output (real income) anymore than output could be omitted from the determination of the price level. We have now analyzed the motives for holding various amounts of money and have brought in the interest cost of holding rather than lending money. The demand and supply of money has been related to the saving-investment analysis of Chapter 5. It should be apparent now that the equilibrium level of real income is determined by four things acting together: the propensity to consume, the marginal efficiency of capital, the demand for money (in real, i.e., purchasing-power terms), and the supply of money (in the same terms). We need to give additional attention now to various explanations of what determines the rate of interest.

CHAPTER **7**

Interest Theory

The literature of monetary theory contains much controversy over what determines the rate of interest. It is natural that monetary theory should be concerned with the cost of obtaining money as well as with the value of it. We have already seen that the interest rate becomes an important variable in our analysis, and we will explore its role further in a later chapter. Here we will review systematically some of the controversy over the determination of the rate of interest.

DETERMINANTS OF THE INTEREST RATE

Prior to the Keynesian *General Theory of Employment, Interest, and Money*,[1] the emphasis had been on two principal elements: time preference, and the marginal productivity of capital. The time-preference

[1] John Maynard Keynes, *The General Theory of Employment, Interest and Money* (New York: Harcourt, Brace & World, 1936).

theory is related to the popular saying that "a bird in the hand is worth two in the bush." Applied to interest, and applied literally, this would imply a very high rate. But the idea is that if one is to be induced to give up present consumption by making someone a loan of money one could have spent, thus postponing the opportunity to consume until later, it would be necessary to compensate him for the postponement. And the strength of people's preference for the bird in the hand (preference for present consumption over future consumption) is said to be an element in the determination of how much interest must be paid to induce someone to save and lend from current income. This would make more sense if people wished to consume all income currently, but mere prudence leads to saving and hence postponing consumption, so interest is not necessary to induce saving. The time-preference factor may still be brought into the picture, however, to explain the amount that people are willing to pay to obtain consumption loans. Buying on installment credit, for instance, requires one to pay interest for the privilege of consuming something now that one's income would allow one to consume only later, but for the loan. How strongly one prefers consuming now instead of waiting until he has saved enough to make the purchase, as of a consumer durable, determines how high a rate of interest he is willing to pay for the privilege. As the volume of consumer loans has increased to substantial proportions in recent years, this element begins to take on importance in the demand for credit. But even here there is not a very strong case, for although the demand for consumer credit varies, its variation does not seem to be due primarily to changes in the cost of the credit (the interest rate). Indeed it seems that few people using consumer credit are aware of the true interest rate they are paying, though they usually have some crude notion, often quite inaccurate, of some of the costs involved.

A more influential theory, and one that must be taken more seriously, is the marginal productivity theory of interest. This theory argues that the long-run equilibrium rate of interest is determined by the marginal productivity of capital. The principal use of borrowed saving is to invest in real capital; the inducement to invest is the expectation that the capital goods will be productive enough to return more than the outlay involved in buying them. The increase in output when more capital is used with given quantities of other factors (or when allowance is made for the effect of any necessary increase in other factors) is called the marginal productivity of the capital. The addition to the total value of the output per year, obtainable by the use of additional capital, sets an upper limit on how much an investor can afford to pay to borrow the money to buy the additional capital goods. Competition between potential investors to get limited funds can force the cost of the funds up to that level. The amount paid per year for each dollar of borrowed funds is the rate of interest paid for the loan. The long-run equilibrium level of the interest rate is thus said to be determined by the marginal productivity of capital.

Keynes introduced quite a twist in the analysis by arguing that the rate of interest was determined only by monetary factors. The amount of new investment in capital goods was said then to adjust to the interest rate, rather than to determine it, as shown in the discussion of the marginal efficiency of capital in Chapter 5. We have also seen that Keynes argued that interest is a reward for parting with liquidity rather than a reward for saving. He thus rejected the earlier theories of interest. And he substituted the notion that the demand for real money (liquidity preference) and the supply of real money determine the rate of interest, as we saw in Chapter 6. This liquidity-preference theory of interest rested on the activity of people buying and selling bonds and thus altering the interest rate when they wanted more liquidity or less liquidity than was provided by the existent money supply.

This picture of interest determination is complicated when one considers, as we did in Chapter 6, the fact that the demand for money is a function of the level of real income as well as of the rate of interest. But the complication is not fatal for a liquidity-preference theory of interest. We simply restrict the analysis to the demand and supply of "idle balances." The total money supply may be thought of as being divided into two parts, active money and idle money. The former is money that circulates as it is used for various money transactions. The latter is money that could be invested in bonds to earn interest, but is held idle instead, at least for the time being. Some of the total stock of money is always required for transactions, the more, the higher the level of income. But the active circulation does not absorb the entire money stock at all times; the remainder is the total supply of idle balances. We do not need to repeat the analysis of the demand for idle balances. The demand and supply of idle balances (of real money) is then said to determine the interest rate, and the mechanism by which this influence operates is that previously described (buying or selling bonds).

This monetary theory of interest did not have the field to itself or battle alone against the "real" interest theories (those ascribing the level of interest to "real" factors: time preference and marginal productivity of capital). A loanable-funds theory of interest also held that monetary factors determined the rate of interest. According to this theory, the rate of interest is determined by the demand and supply of loanable funds. It is the price that equates the quantity of loanable funds demanded with the quantity of loanable funds supplied. It is argued that since the rate of interest is the price of a money loan, it is natural that demand and supply of the funds involved in the loans be considered the important determinants of their price. The demand and supply curves are presumed to be the normal shape, with the quantity of loanable funds supplied rising as the price—which is the inducement to lend—rises, and the quantity of funds people want to borrow declining as the price they must pay for the funds rises. When we look into the components of the demand and supply of loanable funds, saving and investment immediately appear to be the dominant elements. Saving provides most of the supply of loanable funds, and the principal demand for such funds is for investment. But idle money may also be "dishoarded" at times to add to the supply of loanable funds, and new-money creation by commercial banks can add to the supply significantly. On the demand side, an increase in idle balances desired goes in the direction of offsetting, to greater or lesser degree, any augmentation of the supply of loanable funds by dis-hoarding. Some net additions to idle balances may be expected over the long run as income rises. However, changes in money ejected from or added to "hoards" are probably significant chiefly for small net movements in one direction or the other for relatively short periods. The loanable-funds theory makes it possible to take any such movements into account when they are of a noticeable magnitude. More important, it makes it possible to integrate into the analysis the rate at which the money supply is being expanded or contracted by the banking system.

THE VARIETY OF INTEREST RATES

It will be noticed that the discussion has been in terms of "the" interest rate, but the rate of interest one pays on a loan varies not only from time to time, but at any given time differs, depending upon many things. The rate for a long loan is different from that for a short loan; the purpose of the loan makes a difference, as does the security provided the lender in case of default. There are indeed a great variety of interest rates at any given time. We need to know something about the whole structure of interest rates.

Insofar as lenders can shift their funds from one part of the total loan market to another, and borrowers can do likewise, these rates will be tied together and move together. So we could speak of a change in "the" interest rate, meaning a change in the general level of interest rates. This is one interpretation that can be given our simplification of speaking of "the" rate, for the different rates are not independent of one another. Anything changing rates in one part of the loan market tends to affect the rest of the market, or much of it, in due course. If lenders were completely indifferent between different outlets for their funds, and if borrowers were completely indifferent between different ways of borrowing, the variety of interest rates would disappear, leaving a single rate.

But the possibility of a change in that rate itself prevents complete indifference between long-term and short-term loans. If, let's suppose, the long-term and short-term loans carried the same interest rate, but people thought there was a probability that the interest rate would rise in the near future, then borrowers would prefer to borrow for longer terms now, rather than to take out a succession of short-term loans. Lenders, on the other hand, would prefer not to lend funds for a long term at a fixed rate, but rather to make a succession of short loans with returns on the later ones increasing. This preference pattern increases the supply of short-term credit and reduces the demand for it, making the short-term interest rate lower than the long-term rate.

Actual interest payments on loans normally contain some reward for the risk the lender takes in parting with his money. This is sometimes referred to as a risk premium, and the amount involved differs from case to case and particularly between different types of loans. Economists are abstracting from this risk element when they talk about interest theory, for they are trying to explain "pure interest," knowing full well that the different risks of different loans is something to add to the picture afterward.

The very process of making loans—seeing to it that they are properly "serviced" (i.e., interest and principal payments are made when due), paying attention to the changing financial position of the borrower and sometimes "advising" him in decisions he makes that can vitally affect the interest of the lender, as well as closing the loans—all of the various aspects of a lending operation, whenever they apply, involve costs. Interest rates for different types of loans reflect the differences in cost, on the average, for that type of loan.

There are other reasons why lenders are not completely indifferent about the type of loan they make, and why borrowers cannot shift at will between them, or are not indifferent about different types of loans. Legal restrictions on some lending institutions, established usually to protect the ultimate lenders against having their funds put into riskier loans than they would choose, prevent the institution from entering some parts of the loanable-funds market. National banks, for instance, are prohibited from investing in corporation stocks (with minor exceptions). Other institutions are formed for the express purpose of specializing in certain types of loans, as the savings-and-loan associations (providing mortgage credit), or the Federal Land Banks (providing mortgage credit to farmers). On the borrowing side, borrowers may not be able to, or should not if they could, add to their mortgage to buy an automobile. A different type and length of loan is best for the car purchase than is best for the purchase of a house. So the loanable-funds market is to some degree compartmentalized, and different interest rates prevail. Where a previous paragraph indicated that the compartments are not completely isolated from one another, so that to some degree the whole level of rates may change together, we are here seeing that fluidity between sectors of the market is sufficiently restricted, so that changes in one rate relative to another in the total structure are possible.

To the degree that the market is somewhat compartmentalized, the loanable-funds theory finds an additional application. It provides the framework for a simple explanation of the variety of interest rates. The supply and demand for loanable funds in each sector of the market can explain each different interest rate. The theory also provides a framework for discussion of the impact of change in any sector of the market on other sectors through some degree of alteration in the demand and supply of loanable funds in other sectors of the market. The different rates, their degree of independence and of interrelatedness, needs to be explained in some such fashion, even if some one rate is taken for simplicity's sake as "the" rate of interest or as an indicator of the level of rates.

SYNTHESIS OF INTEREST THEORIES

In the opening section of this chapter, we saw how various theories of interest emphasized different factors as responsible for making the rate of interest what it is. Each theory was plausible enough in itself, if carefully stated, for each latched on to some element that is important in determining the rate of interest. The question is whether it is possible to develop a framework into which these different elements can be fitted without involving ourselves in logical inconsistencies. Instead of reviewing all efforts to reconcile the different theories, we shall show how an analytical result already attained can be interpreted to give scope for elements from different theories of interest. Also certain remaining problems of interest theory will be discussed briefly.

In our analysis of the role of money in the Keynesian system (Chapter 6), we started with a simple picture of the demand and supply of money in which variations in interest brought equality between the quantity demanded and the quantity supplied. While some equilibrating role of interest was retained in the final formulation of the Keynesian analysis as pictured in Figure 6.3, we might notice now that we could not say, in the end, that the equilibrium rate of interest was determined only by the demand and supply of money. Indeed, we saw that demand and supply of money determine only certain equilibrium relations between interest and income. In the end, it appears that saving and investment also have something to do with the rate of interest, just as pre-Keynesian, or classical, economists said. A change in the marginal productivity of capital will affect the rate of real investment, shifting the savings-investment curve and altering interest as well as income. Insofar as time preference plays a role, it may be represented as influencing net saving of households, and the effect can be traced similarly in the diagram. A change in the money supply is obviously easy to introduce (shift the money-equilibrium curve to the right for an increase in the money supply). And any net change in loanable funds due to hoarding or dishoarding (that is, the desire to hold idle balances) can similarly be traced by shifting the liquidity preference curve and, consequently, the money equilibrium curve (the latter to the left for hoarding, to the right for dishoarding). Thus the aggregative-equilibrium diagram is one into which the various elements of interest theory discussed in this chapter can be fitted.

It would seem as though the problems of interest theory had been resolved simply, but it is not quite that simple. The argument between proponents of different views persists; we must deal briefly with some further differences. Dispute over the role of real and of monetary factors has been supplemented by dispute over the role of "stocks" and of "flows," and over short-run and long-run equilibrium (not to be confused with short- and long-term loans).

The liquidity-preference theory of interest is a "stock" theory; it says that the rate of interest is determined by the relationship between the total stock of money supplied and the stock of money people demand to hold at the time. The loanable-funds theory is a "flow" theory; it says that the rate of interest is determined by the supply and demand of loanable funds; but these are flows of funds coming into the loan markets in each period of time, and amounts that people are desirous of borrowing per period. The interest rate equilibrates these two flows, just as price in a commodity market influences the rates at which people buy the commodity and the rate of production that supplies the market. Additional quantities of loanable funds come onto the market period after period, and borrowers take funds off the market period after period. The loanable-funds theory looks at these per period rates of supply and demand of new funds. The per period rates of saving and of investment are most important, but are supplemented by per period rates of change in money supply and sometimes by changes in hoarding.

Is interest determined by the equilibrium in the two flows just mentioned, or by equilibrium between the two stocks mentioned? Actually there need be no argument about final equilibrium, as indicated by the aggregative-equilibrium diagram (Figure 6.3); for there the interest rate equilibrates both the market in which the money stocks are involved and the market in which the money flows are involved. The problem that remains is with respect to disequilibrium. Here it is clear that a disturbance in either market, an upset in demand and supply of money equilibrium or in saving-investment equilibrium, will alter the interest rate and also cause an alteration in the final equilibrium balance in the other market. So proponents of both theories are in a sense correct. And the question turns into whether one theory sheds more light on long-run equilibrium and the other on short-run equilibrium.

And at this point we should refer again to the older "real" theories of interest also, for in equilibrium there is equality between the rate of interest and the marginal productivity of capital and presumably the rate of time preference, as well as between the two stocks and two flows treated by monetary-interest theories. The question really becomes which factors adjust most quickly and which most slowly when disequilibrium develops. There is no discussion anymore of the time-preference factor in this connection, possibly because of difficulties in its interpretation or because it can be thought of as being absorbed in a loanable-funds analysis. If interest changes it would at least be possible for them to alter their subsequent rate of saving or of borrowing for consumer purposes. But this is likely to be a small part of the total loanable-funds picture. What is more significant is that not all the flows of funds into and out of loanable-funds markets do adjust rapidly. Saving habits themselves probably do not usually adjust very quickly to changes in the interest rate. Real investment, which is the primary outlet for savings, requires long planning in many cases. Sometimes borrowing is spread over the whole period in execution of the various parts of an investment program; in this case, investment may adjust only very slowly to changed interest rates. It is otherwise with the "stock" equilibrium, in which certain adjustments may be made relatively quickly, even if final adjustment takes longer. If we concern ourselves for the moment with the alternatives of holding bonds or cash, it is apparent that if the interest rate changes, it is possible to shift in or out of bonds quite quickly. Indeed, if the general climate of opinion has been altered, it may require relatively few transactions in bond markets to establish a new equilibrium interest rate again. If we take into account the full range of money substitutes and, particularly, all types of securities, including those growing out of the variety of types of loan transactions, it may take longer for the rates of return obtainable on purchases of all types of old claims, including bonds, to reach a new equilibrium. But returns on outstanding stocks of all kinds of old "claims" (or money-debt instruments and securities) can adjust in security markets more quickly than can the rates at which new funds come on the market or are taken out of it. Thus a liquidity-preference analysis, preferably broadened to include all relevant securities besides bonds, gives a better explanation of factors determining the short-run equilibrium rate of interest, while the loanable-funds analysis gives a better explanation of what determines a longer-run equilibrium rate of interest as well as an explanation of the variety of interest rates on new loans of all types. In the still longer run, the total stock of real capital tends to adjust in such fashion that its marginal productivity equals the rate of interest. One might say that the monetary theories explain the variations of the rate of interest around its very long-run trend, which is explained by the marginal-productivity theory. This is a better way of putting it than to suggest that the long-run equilibrium is generally reached "after a long time," for change doesn't give us much chance to reach one long-run equilibrium position before that will-o'-the-wisp has moved and the chase continued.

The above treatment of the elements of interest

theory should not be taken to indicate that controversy over these matters has been finally resolved. The relative roles of the factors we have considered may continue to be disputed for some time to come.

CHAPTER **8**

Tying in the Price Level

We have explained the equilibrium rate of interest and level of real income in terms of four basic factors: the propensity to consume, the marginal efficiency of capital, liquidity preference, and the real money supply. But no explanation has been given of the price level, comparable to that discussed in Chapters 3 and 4 and found there to have serious shortcomings. It was shown there that attempts to explain price-level behavior in terms of changes in the money supply ran into difficulty when changes in the money supply involved changes in the level of employment and national income. Now that the shortcomings with respect to the income side of the picture have been overcome, it is necessary to see what can be said about the determination of the price level that will be consistent with the income analysis. We can no longer abstract from price-level changes, though our basic concepts must continue to be stated in real terms.

SOME PRICE LEVEL RELATIONSHIPS

Certain crucial relationships involving the price level are indeed implicit in the analysis at this point. To see these and be able to take the next step easily, let us suppose that the economy is in aggregative equilibrium now, and that the four basic factors determining that equilibrium do not change for a time. We must get around to talking about the absolute magnitudes of three variables: the price level, the money supply in dollars, and the money wage rate. The three are not independent of one another. Whatever the absolute values may actually be in the equilibrium situation we are supposing exists, their relative values are implicit in two relationships. We must understand these relationships before we can solve the problem of the absolute levels of these three variables.

Since the particular equilibrium situation we are envisaging was determined partly by a given real money supply, there must be a certain relationship between the price level and the dollar money supply. The actual dollar supply could be anything at all for this level of real income, provided the price level were such that the dollar supply constituted the same real money supply that was involved in this aggregative equilibrium. Or we could say, any absolute price level would be possible with this same real-income level, provided the dollar money supply was exactly what would then be necessary to constitute the real money supply appropriate to this real-income level. If we do indeed have an aggregative equilibrium situation as we have supposed, we will, in fact, find that the price level and the dollar money supply are related to each other as we have suggested they must be for a given equilibrium income. The additional point being made is that their absolute levels could have been different without affecting the equilibrium level of income and interest.

The other relationship to be explored is that between the price level and the level of money wage rates ("the" money wage rate, for short). To discuss this we must bring in two new concepts, one of them a new equilibrium condition, and one a technological factor. It was suggested earlier that short-run changes in the level of real income—the total output of consumer goods and capital goods—represent, primarily, changes in the level of employment. So when we have determined the level of real income, total production, we have determined the level of employment. We need to go further and recognize that production is carried on with a certain technology that determines the input requirements to get certain outputs, and, therefore, the changes in output resulting from changes in inputs. We refer to the set of such relationships as the production function. Though a technological factor, the production function is one of the basic factors for our economic analysis. It determines what level of employment is involved in producing the particular equilibrium level of real income we have supposed existed. It determines also how much output is increased if any input is increased. The additional output from an additional unit of an input is termed the marginal productivity of that factor of production. Applied to labor, we can say the production function determines what the marginal productivity of labor shall be when the level of employment is that required for the supposed existing equilibrium level of real income. The significance of this figure must be given further consideration.

In a private-enterprise economy, firms cannot afford to pay labor (or any factor of production) more than its marginal productivity. If they were to do so they would lose money and, if this were carried too far, they would be forced out of business. In a competitive economy, no factor need accept less than its marginal productivity as its pay; for firms can always increase their profit by increasing their employment of a factor of production up to the very point where the pay to the factor equals its marginal productivity. And if firms compete, competition for factors will force their pay up to the level of their marginal productivity. The tendency, therefore, in a competitive private-enterprise economy is for factors of production to be paid their marginal productivity, and in equilibrium this condition will hold. Where competition prevails, production will continue to change until the condition is met. In other words, this is another equilibrium condition for the economic system. Applied to labor, in our hypothetical situation, the wage rate will be equal to the marginal productivity of labor, whatever that may be with the given technology and given production function, at the equilibrium level of real income or production.

In the preceding paragraph we were talking about the amount of labor employed and the amount by which output is increased by a marginal change in the amount of labor employed. The discussion ran in "real," not in monetary, terms. So it is the "real" wage rate that is referred to in that paragraph as the pay of labor in our situation. Labor will be receiving a money wage which is equivalent, at the existing price level, to that amount of real income. Or, one could say, the price level will be such that, at the existing money wage rate, the real wage rate will be the equilibrium rate, that is, equal to the real marginal productivity of labor. Our aggregative equilibrium implies, therefore, a certain relationship between the price level and the money wage rate. The absolute level of these is a matter of indifference, provided the appropriate relationship is maintained between them. That is, our equilibrium level of employment is consistent with a different level of money wage rates and a different absolute price level, so long as the two maintain such a relationship between them that the real wage rate equals the marginal productivity of labor (defined as above in real terms).

So in aggregative equilibrium, two things are simultaneously related to the price level in a specifiable manner: the dollar money supply, and the money wage rate. In equilibrium the *relative* values of these three are determined. And if the economy now *is* in equilibrium, we will have certain specific *actual* values for these three variables. But we do not yet know why the three are at one absolute level rather than at a higher or lower level (at which the appropriate relative values could still hold). In exploring this question, we enter a murky area in which there are, as yet, no heavily traveled and hence well-beaten paths to our destination.

PASSIVE AND ACTIVE VARIABLES

Since the supply of dollars, the price level, and the money wage rate are related in equilibrium, whatever helps determine the equilibrium value of any one of them, helps determine the equilibrium value of all three. The quantity theory, without examining in detail what made the dollar money supply change, took this as the independent variable and tried to establish how the price level would passively adjust and what relationship it would maintain to the money supply. When a quantity theorist said that the price level would change in proportion to the money supply, he was, in effect, saying that the real money supply would not change. We have seen that the real money supply is indeed different for different levels of employment and real income.

We have made progress in ascertaining the nature of the equilibrium relationship between the dollar supply and the price level, and in learning how employment and the real money supply are related. The question remains whether change in the dollar supply, somehow explained, is the active factor producing changes in price level and, we now add, in money wage rates; or whether the dollar money supply changes passively as a result of changes in one of the other two. Clearly, an independent change in the dollar supply could be an active factor disrupting an equilibrium situation. It could cause a change in the values of the other two variables; they might change in a way that would be consistent with maintaining the equilibrium (or rather, restoring the same employment equilibrium). Actually, an independent change in the dollar supply might lead to reactions other than restoring the same employment equilibrium with the appropriate new wage and price levels. But at the moment, we are attempting to bring out only the possibility that the dollar supply factor might play either an active or a passive role. It can change independently of a change in the price and wage level. Are most of the changes in our trio of interrelated variables initiated thus, or does the dollar money supply play a more passive role?

If we go behind the actual changes in the dollar supply, we find that the principal role of monetary authorities has been to ensure a growth in the monetary reserve base sufficient to facilitate growth of dollars to finance a growing national income. But we find that the principal factor inducing bank credit to expand or contract is a change in the rate of real investment (not financed by changes in current saving). This takes us back to changing marginal efficiency of capital, and to the consequent changes in real income and in the demand for bank credit. What looks like an active role for the dollar supply may thus, in many cases, be traceable to something else. When we examine the forces of economic change, the money supply often appears to be a passive factor after all. Such passive changes don't explain "the starting point" or absolute level from which changes occur, and perhaps the best we can do is regard this as a sort of "historical accident." So while we can contend that the dollar supply can, at times, be the active factor, we are not able to make a strong case that it normally is. For a better case, we should probably turn to situations in which a government inflates the money supply so rapidly, to cover rising outlays, as to generate rapid inflation. In a normal economy, the money supply adjusts to needs rather than dominating the picture.

Another leading contender for the title of dominant variable today is the money wage rate. Changes in the money wage rate are brought about in the collective-bargaining process in a significant portion of the economy and set patterns that influence other wages. The view is widely held that this process initiates changes in the price level. There is little room for doubt that it can do so. This can certainly be the active factor to which the equilibrium values of the other factors adjust. And other changes in the economy may result if the dollar money supply and price level do not passively move to their new equilibrium values. It is not so easy to establish whether or not the money wage rate changes do indeed govern the other factors all the time. There is room to show that the money wage rate can also be a passive factor at times. Indeed, it is fairly clear that business firms vary in their willingness to grant wage increases under pressure. There are times when they feel they can either absorb a wage increase or, more likely, can pass it along to consumers in higher prices. In such cases, a given degree of aggressiveness on the part of those seeking higher wages will lead to bigger wage increases than in some other circumstances. There are other times when business fears it cannot handle big wage increases without serious adverse consequences for itself, and it manages to hold the line on wage rates. Labor-union leaders, for their part, recognize differences in the situation and vary their demands as well as the amount of pressure behind them for wage increases. The behavior of the price level is itself one of the factors considered by both labor and business. Labor clearly steps up its demand for wage increases when there is price inflation—they demand cost-of-living increments. So there is a case for considering the money wage rate, to some degree and at times, as a passive factor rather than the one that dominates the picture and calls the tune to which all else adjusts. With this said, however, it appears that changes in the money wage rate should probably be regarded as more commonly the active factor than changes in the money supply, as our economy works nowadays. The money wage rate is determined largely in a process with which we are familiar—the collective-bargaining process. The equilibrium price level is determined as a result, and the dollar money supply that that price level requires is determined also. In general, the price level and the dollar supply are the more passive variables, though the nature of the causal relations can be and sometimes is more complicated than this.

THE ROLE OF INSTITUTIONAL FACTORS

When we talk about collective bargaining over wages, we are discussing what may be termed an institutional factor. When we speak of the powers of the Federal

Reserve to control reserves of the banking system, we are dealing with an institutional factor. We saw the first of these factors involved in the determination of the money wage rate, and the second involved in the determination of the dollar money supply. It is natural to suppose that the set of economic institutions and the institutionalized ways of doing things in any country would have an important bearing on how the economy operates and an important place in the explanation of its operation. Are there other institutional factors that should be brought into our monetary theory? In particular, how far can they go in explaining the price level?

The analysis thus far has continued to treat the price level as a purely passive factor. It was taken as adjusting to other factors in each of the theories, with a single exception. What was dubbed a "contra-quantity theory" approach attributed to a banker was presented briefly as a possible view, but no explanation was given at that time as to what determines P when M is just passive. It would be possible for the price level to be the active factor in the trio we have been discussing in this chapter if there are independent forces operating directly upon P and not only affecting it indirectly through an impact on other variables. Let us consider what institutional factors might have an important direct bearing upon the behavior of the price level. Three categories of institutional influence will be mentioned.

The first is custom. In some economies, this would indeed be a dominant factor in determining prices. In an economy as dynamic as ours, and one in which the general price level has been under such pressure as is occasioned by major wars, the force of custom has been reduced to minimal proportions. But the human animal remains a creature of habit, and this introduces a resistance to change in prices that makes for greater "stickiness" of the price level than would otherwise be the case. Instead of helping explain price-level movements, this explains some degree of sluggishness in movement.

Government is the second factor to be considered. We are concerned here not with the impact of monetary-fiscal policy upon the price level, for this operates through its impact on aggregate demand. We are looking now for any ways in which government policies directly affect important segments of the price level. To begin with, government regulatory commissions can be said to fix public utility rates. These are important prices, and as such enter both directly and indirectly (as costs of producing some things) into the price index. The agricultural price-support program is another instance where government influences important prices. In this case, government maintains some prices at levels above what the market would set. Where resale price maintenance laws are effective, government gives private interests the power to enforce certain prices, privately set. Enforcement of anti-trust laws may lower some prices. Indirectly, some prices may be affected by minimum-wage legislation, by the government's role in labor disputes, or by changes in social-security legislation. Excise taxes that are directly added to product prices are relevant here also, though the effect of taxes in general on aggregate demand is not being considered here. To evaluate the direct effect of government action on the price level, it is necessary to consider separately each such action to see whether it can be considered to be a factor introducing independent changes in the price level. We might also see whether it is a response to changes whose effect it is damping, or whether it plays any other role with respect to prices.

Finally, we will look briefly at business structure and policy. Can the price level be affected by the degree of concentration or monopoly in the economy, and the pricing policies of business generally? A change in either of these could, conceivably, produce a change in the behavior of the price level. Prices in highly competitive markets generally fluctuate more in the face of economic changes than prices in other markets. Also, a decline in the amount of competition in a market is likely to lead to higher prices in that market than otherwise. Indeed, since business firms set the prices on the things they produce, it might seem that all one needs to explain the price level is business pricing policies. The price level is what these policies make it, and a change in policy leads to a change in price level. It should be admitted that this can be an active factor in the picture, impinging on the price level. But when one gets specific about what business pricing policies are, what is meant by a change in them, and how they work out, this approach is not so enlightening as sometimes is claimed. To begin with, it is commonly said that the way business firms set prices is on a cost-plus-markup basis; this is all right as far as it goes, but it doesn't get behind the costs. These costs, for most firms, include many prices of intermediate products, as a glance at any inter-industry relations table will quickly show. So the explanation, rather than giving a real answer, largely passes the buck. Changes in policy turn out to mean, primarily, changes in the markup decided upon.

But precisely here it becomes clear that the decision is not really independent of the general economic situation after all. Margins are not arbitrarily widened or narrowed, but fixed in relation to economic forecasts. Business price policy can exert some independent influence, but it does not operate in a vacuum impervious to the other factors we have been discussing, including the behavior of the money supply. Indeed, one function of business management is to ascertain the behavior of all the factors we have discussed and to decide how best to adjust the firm's behavior to them. Its role is partly passive.

We are thus unable to establish the case for a price level determined directly by institutional factors, apart from the other factors we have discussed. What we find is that institutional factors can have a significant impact upon the behavior of the price level. Some have a direct effect on some groups of prices. Some have an effect through their influence on wage rates and some through their influence on the money supply, or through other indirect routes. But the institutional factors operate differently in different economic situations.

We conclude that we can best speak of an interaction between institutional and other factors. If, for example, collective bargaining over wage rates takes place in a setting in which the money supply is unlikely to expand, the outcome and the consequent impact on the price level is likely to be different from what it would be if the money supply responded passively or was itself actively raising the price level.

CHAPTER **9**

Keynesian and Classical Views

Our study of monetary theory that began with the quantity approach shifted, upon discovering shortcomings, to an income-expenditure approach derived primarily from Keynes. In analyzing changes in the price level, the quantity approach failed to take sufficient account of changes in real income. The Keynesian approach typically concentrates so heavily on real income that the price level gets inadequate attention. Chapter 8 did get us back to the price level again and to the dollar money supply. It also brought in the money wage rate. But it did not establish any necessary relation between these money variables and the level of real income or the interest rate. The relation of the two sets of variables appeared to be a historical accident and essentially arbitrary. But are they really independent and without influence on each other? What sort of an adjustment does a change within one set of variables produce? Our last two chapters will concern themselves with some of these interrelations. In this chapter, we will compare further the Keynesian views and pre-Keynesian, or classical, views. This will make clearer the basic points of difference and help us consider what more we can or cannot take from the older classical approach, of which the quantity theory was a part.

BEHIND SAY'S LAW

It is ordinarily said that the quantity theory assumed full employment as did much of classical economics. It is possible, as pointed out earlier, to make a relatively simple statement of the effect of M on P if T (defined as real income, or total output) is taken as a constant. Typical formulations of the quantity theory logically implied that a change in the money supply would not affect real income (or at least not the V/T ratio). Yet it was precisely at this point, in not taking adequate account of the significance of different levels of real income (and of changes in the level), that the quantity theory's weakness became fatal to any simple formulation of the theory. The question is why T was handled in the fashion it was—it might have been merely for the sake of simplicity. We can be sure that the classical economists did not merely assume T constant at a full-employment level because they never saw any unemployment. Rather, their general economic analysis had led them to adopt Say's Law as valid.

Jean Baptiste Say was a French economist who argued that a money economy was not fundamentally different from a barter economy, in that the total supply of goods produced was identical with the total demand for goods. Money was treated as a medium of exchange and not as a store of value. There was no allowance in this view for people to sell and then hold the cash idle instead of buying with it. It was supposed that anyone who produced something to sell did so simply to get money to buy something else. This seemed to rule out the possibility that Keynes later made central in his thinking, namely, that there could, at times, be a deficiency of aggregate demand, leading to unemployment. If the total demand for goods was the same as the total supply there would be no such problem. But how could the classical economists be sure Say was right? There was unemployment at times, but it might be due to something other than a shortage of demand. It might be due to various types of economic change that temporarily cause unemployment as the economy readjusts. The question was what, if anything, ensured that the *equilibrium* level of real income would be that point at which there was full employment of the labor force.

One word provides the classical answer to that question—"competition." Competitive mechanisms in the economy were relied upon to make the economy tend toward a full-employment equilibrium level of production. With the assurance that these mechanisms normally worked, the classical economists were warranted in accepting Say's Law and formulating their monetary theory for a condition of full employment. We shall not spell out the analysis of the role of competition fully, but do need to look at two parts of the analysis that concern monetary factors.

THE ROLE OF THE INTEREST RATE

The problem for anyone holding Say's Law was presented by the obvious fact of saving. The classical answer was that saving is just another way of spending the money. The answer isn't so obvious, but it referred to the fact that the investment of savings involves the purchase of capital goods, in the last analysis, instead of consumer goods. But what about the possibility, which we have already discussed, that the amount that leaks out of the money-income stream in saving would not all be injected back into the stream by real investment? The answer given was "competition." For, it was said, people will not save if they cannot earn interest on their saving, nor save as much at low as at high rates of interest. And those buying capital goods with savings will buy more such goods if the rate of interest that they have to pay for the savings is low than if it is high. The rate of interest will be adjusted by competition among savers or investors to equalize the amount people are willing to save and the amount people are willing to invest. Then there can be no net leakage from the income stream; aggregate demand will equal aggregate supply, and Say's Law will hold. Monetary theory can then treat T as constant at a full employment level. There may be changes from time to time in the rate of saving and investment, but all they alter is the proportion of production that consists of capital goods rather than consumer goods; there is no change in the equilibrium level of production and employment.

This may be illustrated by Figure 9.1. The saving

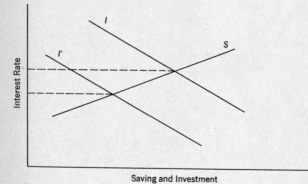

Figure 9.1. The Classical View.

(S) and investment (I) curves show how those variables were supposed to vary with the rate of interest. The problem could arise from either an increase in the propensity to save or a decrease in the opportunities for profitable investment. The latter has been illustrated in Figure 9.1 by shifting the investment curve to the left. At the previous equilibrium rate of interest, there is an excess of saving over investment as a result. Competition between savers was supposed to reduce interest to a new equilibrium rate. The drop in the interest rate reduces the rate of saving and stimulates investment to produce a new equilibrium. Although investment is below the original equilibrium level, saving is lower also (hence consumption is higher); so there is no net leakage, and output remains at the original full employment level (T is unchanged).

What did Keynes find wrong with this analysis? He contended that although the economy might sometimes work this way for small changes, it sometimes failed to do so for large changes. His reason was that saving and investment are not as responsive to changes in the rate of interest as the classical view supposes. On the basis of this charge, among others, he rejected Say's Law. Keynes would redraw the diagram so that it would appear as it does in Figure 9.2, with both

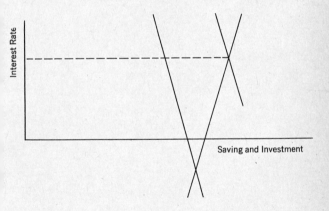

Figure 9.2. The Keynesian View.

saving and investment responding only slightly to changes in the rate of interest. So when the investment curve shifts to the left, representing a worsening of real investment prospects, there may be no positive interest rate at which savings and investment can be equated. People are not going to pay others interest to borrow money from them (which is what negative interest rates would imply). At positive interest rates, saving continues to exceed investment. This net leakage from the income stream reduces money and real income, and this continues until they are again equal at some lower income level. But equilibrium is achieved with less than full employment. That equilibrium might be so low that there is zero saving and zero investment. Or, if the decline did not cumulate to that point, it might be that equilibrium would be restored as indicated by the multiplier analysis, with k applied to the initial decline in the rate of investment (before saving declined). The Keynesian view can be stated roughly by saying that saving and investment are equalized not by changes in the rate of interest, in such cases, but by changes in the level of real income and employment. Income falls so low that people cannot save more than business firms are willing to invest in real capital goods, and then the decline stops.

The dispute between Keynesian and classical views here turns out to be a dispute over facts. As such, an empirical investigation should be able to settle the dispute. For one side asserts that savers and investors are quite responsive to changes in the rate of interest, and the other says that they are not. Figures 9.1 and 9.2 show how different the consequences are in the two cases. If the classical view about people's actual reactions to interest-rate changes is correct, flexibility of interest rates should be able to correct unemployment, even when the profitability of investment drops off. If market competition does not automatically flex the interest rate enough, a central bank should be able, through monetary policy alone, to cure a depression, if not to prevent it from developing. Thus the implications of the difference in views are quite significant for policy. The relative impotence of monetary policy in depression casts much doubt upon the classical view. Empirical research is not yet extensive enough to permit a complete statement on the interest elasticity of saving and investment functions. Apparently some types of investment are more responsive to changes in interest than others. In general, however, the Keynesian view as to what the facts are seems to be closer to the truth. People save because it is prudent, and the cyclical variations of interest seem to influence S less than does the variation in real income. Investors, for their part, seem to be influenced much more by other factors. So cyclical variations of interest rates, while having some influence, are relatively minor. If this view of the facts continues to be borne out in the future, we are warranted in taking the Keynesian rather than the classical view.

THE MONETARY EFFECT OF WAGE COMPETITION

There was another way in which the classical view supported the contention that competition would lead the economy to full-employment equilibrium. The argument was that if unemployment existed, competition in the labor market would continue until full employment was reached. This rested on the principle of diminishing marginal productivity of labor, and the proposition that a firm would hire labor only up to the point where the wage equaled the marginal productivity of labor. If the wage rate is higher than the marginal productivity of labor when all laborers wanting jobs are employed, then either the wage rate must come down to that level, or unemployment will grow until the marginal productivity of those employed equals the wage. The marginal-productivity curve of labor, stated in terms of the value of the additional output, rather than in physical terms, is treated as the demand curve for labor as a whole, as shown in Figure 9.3.

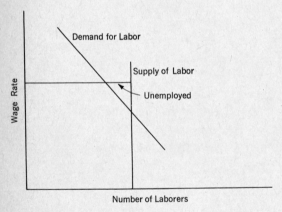

Figure 9.3. Aggregate Demand-and-Supply Curves for Labor, Classical View.

This analysis is very appealing to many today, because it implies that unemployment is due to wage rates being too high, and that cutting wages is the simple and obvious cure for depression. Nonetheless, the analysis is erroneous. A demand curve for labor can be used this way when dealing with any single firm, and probably for any one industry. But when applied to the whole economy, circular reasoning is involved. When a demand curve is drawn, what is said is that the quantity demanded (of whatever it is) increases as its price falls, *caeteris paribus*. And the other things that must be supposed not to change by a decline in the price of the item in question include the prices of related goods and people's incomes. When dealing with demand curves for labor, one can correctly argue that a decline in the wage rate in a firm will not appreciably affect the purchasing power of the firm's customers and, hence, will not adversely affect its sales. If demand for the product is unchanged, then at lower wage rates it can indeed afford to hire more employees, increase supply, and move further down on the demand curve for its product. But when one draws a demand curve for labor as a whole, it is not legitimate to assume that a cut in the wage rate will not affect the demand for goods as a whole. Whether a wage cut raises demand, lowers it, or leaves it unchanged depends upon whether total wages paid out increase, decrease, or remain unchanged. That is a matter of whether employment increases more or less than in the same proportion as wages are cut. One must therefore know to what degree employment will be affected in order to draw the aggregate demand for labor curve in the first place. One cannot therefore simply derive this quantity from the demand curve. That is to say, one is involved in circular reasoning in using an aggregate demand curve for labor to argue that a general wage cut will increase employment.

The same sort of circular reasoning is used by those who argue that an increase in the wage rate will cure unemployment by increasing purchasing power. It is not so easy to determine the aggregative effects of wage changes.

But the classical view that wage competition ensured full-employment equilibrium has been revived in more sophisticated form by A. C. Pigou and others. It is argued that, if the dollar money supply is kept constant, competition in an economy with unemployment will bring down money wage rates and also the general price level. That is, unemployed workers, if allowed to compete for available jobs, will offer to work for less than the going rate, thus bringing down wage rates. As costs of production fall, competition between firms will bring their prices down along with their costs. The net result will be that the purchasing power of the dollar will be increased. If now people have the same number of dollars as before, their liquid wealth will be increased. We could say that an increase in the real money supply had been brought about by the drop in the price level. This is said to lead them to save less and to spend more on consumption. And this in turn should increase production and employment.

Keynes rejected the view that wage competition could be counted upon to increase employment, although he conceded the possibility in some circumstances. He started also from the contention that, if wages fall, prices would fall also, if there was enough competition. He then supposed that people whose real money balances had been thus increased would buy bonds with the "extra money" if the interest rate was not too low. This would lower the interest rate and possibly increase real investment. But the relative inelasticity of investment to interest changes, and the possibility that interest might fall so low that no further "leverage" could be exerted by this method, led Keynes to turn his back upon the wage-competition angle. He failed to take into account the possibility that, as the lower price level made people's money balances into bigger "real balances," they might spend more on goods. This appears to be a surprising oversight; for the quantity theory, which Keynes had taught for years before he worked out his own theory, rested upon the use of any extra cash to buy goods. And surely this alternative is open to people.

What shall we say of this difference between Keynesian and classical views? Pigou is correct that there is some price level in any depression low enough that, if the money supply is not allowed to fall, people's real balances would be large enough to induce the additional spending needed to restore full employment. There is some price level that, for any money balance one holds, would make it so large in purchasing power terms that one would have no need to save out of income again. This is the kernel of truth in the Pigouvian argument. If wage and price competition is pushed relentlessly, wage rates and the general price level might conceivably be forced low enough to eliminate saving, or to cause dissaving if need be, in order to get back to full employment. An economy so competitive would have equilibrium only at full employment. For with anything less, the deflationary proc-

ess would, we suppose, not be able to stop. Keynes
failed to see that competition of this sort undercut his
idea that a competitive economy could be in equilibrium with less than full employment. How important is this logical flaw in the Keynesian analysis?
How devastating has this new classical attack on the
Keynesian analysis been? We might say, in the words
of Alvin Hansen, that it has amounted to an anemic
counterrevolution. The discussion of the "Pigou effect," as it has been called, has been extensive, but only
a fragment of it can be summarized here.

Some consideration must be given to the question
of what monetary and other assets can be expected
to increase in value and lead to an increase in spending
as a result of wage-and-price deflation. This leads
directly to consideration of the effect of such deflation on debts and debtors. A substantial portion of the
money supply is matched by debt of private borrowers
to the bank, and the adverse effect on those who have
to pay back these loans offsets the favorable impact
on those who now hold the money created by the
loans. The burden of other debts will also be increased.
Deflation to cure depression simply widens the trail
of bankruptcies. It seems very doubtful that in a period
of bankruptcy, characterized by falling wages and
prices and increasing unemployment, the aggregative-
consumption function can be raised by the fact that
some part of the money supply now represents a net
increase in purchasing power for somebody. The impact of greater deflationary pressure from increased
competition is, in such a setting, going to create such

adverse expectations as to make matters worse, and extend the deflationary process. It is for this reason that Keynesians argue that the stickiness of wages and prices is a stabilizing rather than a destabilizing factor in the economy. The cumulative downward spiral does not go so far, if the wage and price level are relatively inflexible downwards, as it does if unremitting competition takes over and continues as long as there is unemployment.

It is generally admitted that the Pigou effect is at best rather weak as a device to push the economy to a full-employment equilibrium. And it can be argued that it is the hardest way, even when it works its best, to achieve a normal objective of monetary policy. The Pigou analysis relies upon the stimulus achievable by increasing the real money supply. But it achieves this by keeping the dollar supply fixed, while lowering the demand for dollars through the slow and painful process of lowering the price and wage level. Monetary policy normally achieves the same increase in the real money supply by leaving the wage and price level alone, and simply increasing the supply of dollars. This can provide at least some stimulus, though it too is limited in a depression. But in this case the stimulus is not so applied as to generate offsetting adverse effects. Pigou himself did not offer the analysis to provide a realistic way of curing depressions in general; and we can safely say that we have not found in this new classical view anything that warrants our going back to monetary analysis resting upon full employment (and constant T) assumptions.

MONETARY AND FISCAL POLICY

In the preceding parts of this chapter, we have seen how disputes over theories about how the economy operates, and in particular over whether it tends toward a full-employment equilibrium output, lead easily into disputes over economic policies. In this section, we shall look briefly at a few more policy matters and at the underlying monetary theory. The multiplier analysis developed earlier is applicable to changes in government expenditures and taxes, with certain modifications in some cases. The principles are the same when a more complicated formula is called for.[1] Such ap-

---

[1] For those who are interested, multipliers for changes in taxes and government expenditures may be developed in the following manner. Treat consumption as a normal function of disposable income, that is, national income minus taxes and plus transfer payments (payments such as social security payments from government, which are not payments for current production). This relation may be written:

$$C = a + b(Y - T_x + T_r)$$

To keep our illustration from becoming too complex, we shall treat transfer payments as a constant and suppose that taxes vary from a fixed level in proportion to income. The tax relation may be written:

$$T_x = T_o + cY$$

These two relations need to be inserted into the income equation with government expenditures (excluding transfer payments) as one component of real income.

$$Y = C + I + G$$

This involves valuing the product of government at its cost, that is, government expenditure. When we substitute the expression of T_x in the consumption function, and the latter in the income equation, we obtain the following equation:

$$Y = a + b(Y - T_o - cY + T_r) + I + G$$

Multiplying and collecting the Y terms on the left produces the following:

$$Y - bY + bcY = a - bT_o + bT_r + I + G$$

plications of the theory are, of course, quite relevant to discussions of the use of fiscal policy to deal with business cycles. It was Keynes's advocacy of deficit spending by government to cure the unemployment of depression that led to the hottest opposition to Keynesian economics.

It should not be surprising that adherents of the quantity theory of money should think largely in terms of monetary policy to stabilize the economy, nor that adherents of Keynesian (income-expenditure) theories should think largely in terms of fiscal policy to stabilize the economy. One relies on changing the volume of money and, sometimes more broadly, liquid assets; the other relies on changing people's income. Which way is more effective in controlling spending? The first thing that can be said easily is that, for the size changes that can readily be made in people's cash balances and in their incomes, the reaction to income changes is

---

Solving for Y yields:

$$Y = \frac{1}{1 - b + bc}(a - bT_o + bT_r + I + G)$$

Our new multiplier formula, taking into account government taxes and transfer payments, is then

$$\frac{1}{1 - b + bc}$$

The b is the marginal propensity to consume. The c is the marginal tax rate. This multiplier applies directly to any term in the parentheses in the final equation. It should be noted that for a tax increase, the income change would be negative, and for both a change in the basic tax (T_o) and the transfer payment (T_r), the change in income will involve the multiplier times b, since it is part of the term in the parentheses. The effect of either of these two changes would be less than the effect of a change in I or G because the b is less than unity. If $b = 90$ percent and $c = 20$ percent, the multiplier would be about 3.57.

much more pronounced than the reaction to changes in money or liquid assets. This of itself is sufficient to imply that fiscal policy is a more powerful tool of economic control than is monetary policy. This conclusion does not need to be modified substantially even when we take into account the impact of monetary policy on interest rates, since saving and investment are not highly interest-elastic.

Monetary policy is of unequal effectiveness in inflation and deflation. It is least effective in curing depression; when the marginal efficiency of capital is low, a lowering of the interest rate, while moving in the right direction, cannot be expected to have as much impact as a direct increase in spending. If, for example, the government increases its outlays, or if it reduces taxes and households increase their outlays, business sales will rise, and the marginal efficiency of capital will be improved. The monetary authorities can make the banks more liquid and enable them to lend, and this is desirable and may even be a precondition of recovery. But until the marginal efficiency of capital improves enough so that business seeks more bank credit, or until business sales and profits increase enough so that banks are willing to lend to them, the excess reserves may lie idle. Even increasing liquidity of the public by open-market purchases on the part of the Federal Reserve may serve largely to satisfy a desire for more liquidity, without producing much new spending.

The way to increase production is to increase business sales; the way to do that is to increase spending by someone. The way to increase spending is to increase the income out of which spending comes, not just temporary cash balances. When business investment declines, incomes of the public can most readily be increased by government outlays or tax reductions, with the ensuing multiplier effects of either. This does produce a government deficit. The magnitude of the effect depends on how the deficit is financed. If the government covers the deficit by selling securities to the general public, it is reducing the liquidity of the buyer; there is at least the possibility that this may reduce what the buyer would otherwise have spent on goods, services, or private securities. If sold to banks, some funds might be tapped that might otherwise have been lent. The greatest stimulus from the deficit would result if it is financed through the central bank. This normally has to be done indirectly through its buying securities in the open market to offset new issue sales by the government. It thus becomes apparent, from a discussion of monetary and fiscal policy dealing with unemployment, that, although fiscal policy is much the stronger, monetary policy is not a matter of indifference. It needs to be coordinated with fiscal policy.

With respect to inflation, it is here that monetary policy has its greater strength, although not at the outset. Monetary authorities, if properly empowered, can indeed halt the growth of the money supply, if need be, to check inflation. This is not fully effective in restraining spending at first because, under the impact of an inflationary situation, it may be possible for (and indeed there is an inducement for) people to carry smaller cash balances, on the average. Thus the velocity of money increases for a time. But the fact is, there are limits to the amount velocity will increase for any "normal" price inflation, that is, for something less than the hyperinflation that produces a flight from the currency. So in the end, monetary policy can be more effective in putting the brakes on an ordinary inflation than in reversing a deflation. Tight money in inflation also produces high interest rates, as the supply of loanable funds is restricted. The policy mix for inflation must consider this and short-run problems also. Fiscal policies for inflation, higher taxes, or lower governmental expenditures, of course, do affect income and expenditures directly, and can thus be quite effective. Indeed, they may be preferable to trying to squeeze cash balances to a minimum, though absence of any monetary restriction is not as good as coordinating monetary and fiscal policies in inflation.

The classical view was that the economy would automatically maintain stability at full employment, through competition, or require only monetary policy. The Keynesian view sometimes seems to assume implicitly that the money wage rate, the price level, and the dollar money supply automatically remain in their appropriate equilibrium relationships, or will do so if fiscal policy is used to maintain stability at full employment. Both faiths in automaticity are misplaced. We have already seen that this is so with respect to the classical employment theory, which had to be corrected and supplemented by elements of the Keynesian analysis. The Keynesian faith is also misplaced, and must be corrected and supplemented by borrowing something still valid from the classical view.

Despite errors, the classical view yielded some insight into the consequences of disequilibrium between the money wage rate, the price level, and the dollar money supply. We cannot assume any automatic short-run equilibrium among them. We saw in Chapter 8 that there are various institutional factors that can impede adjustment of the price level or can introduce pressure on it to change independently of the dollar supply or the money wage. We know that if a change in one of these three factors occurs, failure of the other two to maintain the previous equilibrium relationships will imply either a change in the real money supply or in the real wage rate. We have recognized that the former change would lead to alteration of the level of employment and real income. The classical view made much of the possible effect of a change in the real wage rate on employment. As we have seen, the specific lines of reasoning were sometimes unsound. Yet it is not to be denied, though sometimes overlooked by Keynesians, that changes in the money wage rate relative to the price level affect the expectations of businessmen; hence, they affect the marginal efficiency of capital, and thereby the rate of investment, and the level of employment and real income. Fiscal policy may not be all that needs to be considered in the event of relations among our final trio of variables that are not compatible with stable full-employment equilibrium. Control of the dollar money supply is faced with the question of when to respond passively to the others, and when and how much to try to stimulate or restrain. The whole set of problems and policy questions raised by disequilibrium within the trio is very complicated and cannot be pursued very far in this book.

CHAPTER **10**

The Behavior of Employment and Prices

We have shown that, in our imperfectly competitive economy, the equilibrium level of real income and employment is determined by the real money supply and three sets of behavioral factors designated by the following terms: propensity to consume and save, marginal efficiency of capital, and liquidity preference. This equilibrium level appeared to be consistent with various levels for three other variables, money wage rate, price level, and dollar money supply, provided the three are in certain relationships to one another. We then explored the possible consequences of changing one or another of the three to affect real income. We want to inquire now how two variables, the price level and real income and employment, behave with respect to each other over time. We shall draw on what we have shown thus far to help to explain this relationship.

AN OUTPUT-PRICE LEVEL RELATIONSHIP

Starting from the low point of the business cycle, the typical relationship between the price level and real income and employment is as shown in Figure 10.1. As aggregate demand increases (i.e., total spend-

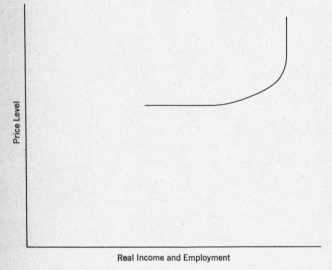

Real Income and Employment

Figure 10.1. An Aggregate Output-Price Level Relationship.

ing for goods and services of all types by all types of spending units), we move to the right on the diagram. Such an increase can be brought about by government deficit spending (through tax reduction or increasing government expenditures) or by a revival in the rate of real investment. The latter, in any case, normal takes over at some point in the upswing of the cycl The diagram shows that the response is initially fe in the reduction of unemployment and the rise in th rate of production; that is, real income increases i proportion to the rise in spending. This is what th earlier multiplier analysis showed resulting from an new injections into the income stream.

The vertical portion of the curve at the right side of the diagram represents the results if aggregate de mand continues to increase after the economy has reached full employment. Not every upswing of the cycle rides up this vertical slope, or even up to the point of full employment. Full-employment income is by definition that level of real income that is the maximum attainable at the time, given full employment and available technology. To be sure, the limit is not quite so absolute as this presumes, but it is not necessary to go into the question of the amount that the maximum can be expanded under some circumstances. The point is that, in general, an increase in aggregate demand beyond what is considered normal full employment is inflationary. The price level increases without appreciable increase in output. This has been where the quantity theory of money found its most useful application.

Well before full employment is reached, the price level begins to rise, along with the increase in output, on the upswing of the business cycle. At first, the price level rises more slowly than output, then later more rapidly. When we approach full employment, most of the effect of any further stimulus to the economy,

the stimulus is an increase in the money supply
ncrease in aggregate demand, spends itself in an
in the price level and relatively little in an in-
n output.

w do we explain the shape of this middle phase
curve? Why does the price level rise with in-
g output before full employment is reached?
are quite a number of factors involved, of which
ollowing may be mentioned here. First, there is
nnological factor. Increasing production may at
point involve increasing the ratio of labor to
of the other factors of production, notably cap-
and consequently diminishing returns, diminish-
marginal productivity. With fixed wage rates this
raise costs of production and will normally lead to
e increases to cover the increased costs. Moreover,
en production is increased, firms will, insofar as
sible, reemploy the most productive workers first.
e closer to full employment the economy moves, the
ser we come to scraping the bottom of the barrel of
e labor supply; the labor taken on is less efficient
an the average, again raising average production
sts, and thereby prices. We have spoken of full em-
loyment as the point where output can increase no
urther, and hence as the point where increased demand merely raises prices. But capacity production is
not reached in all sectors of the economy simultaneously. In some industries or firms, the existent capacity
s fully utilized before it is in others, and the labor
vailable is fully employed before it is in others. In
ese industries, prices rise while other industries are
ill able to increase output. To be sure, in the long

run, capacity can be increased anywhere, but we are talking about the short run. In the short run, the closer the economy comes to the full-employment mark, the more industries run into "bottlenecks," that is, into operating at full capacity with additional pressure merely forcing up certain prices. So the closer to full employment the economy moves, the more bottlenecks and the larger the number of sectors of the economy where the price level is forced up.

In addition to such technological factors, there are a number of what we earlier termed institutional factors. The better the general business situation, the larger the number of firms that may take advantage of it by pricing policies designed to increase their profit margin. And certainly, the lower the level of unemployment and the better the business profits (as well as the higher the price level), the more pressure will be generated by labor unions to force up wage rates. As conditions get progressively better, the resistance to these pressures becomes less, and the wage increases tend to be passed on in price increases. To be sure, only the wage increases that exceed productivity increases raise labor costs and put upward pressure on prices. But the productivity factor may not be taken fully into account, at times, in passing along a wage increase in higher prices.

The curve we have drawn is sometimes called the aggregate-supply curve, because it relates the price level and aggregate output. But it is necessary to realize that the proper interpretation of this curve is quite different from that of an ordinary supply curve in microeconomics. There, a rising supply curve is normally interpreted to mean that a higher price level induces an increase in production. In Figure 10.1, the price level is the dependent, not the independent variable. When aggregate output increases, the price level rises to the degree indicated by the curve. At first it does not rise at all, because, as we pointed out earlier in connection with the multiplier analysis, firms normally respond to a rise in sales by increasing production— rather than keeping output fixed and raising prices. For further increases in output, we found that technological and institutional factors lead to prices rising, and rising faster the closer the economy moves to full employment. When output can't be substantially increased in the short run by further increases in aggregate demand, such demand increase produces a sharp rise in the price level.

It may be noted that just as aggregate supply is not to be interpreted in a manner analogous to that of supply in microeconomic analysis, the same may be said of aggregate demand. It is not to be thought of as represented by a downward sloping curve showing that people will buy more output the lower the price level. For, as we saw when discussing wage competition at the aggregate level, the amount people buy depends in large measure upon the amount of production and employment, rather than being entirely independent of it. The price level is, as we now see, a function of the level of production and is not the independent variable in this analysis.

So, at the aggregate level, we do not draw the usual shaped curves showing demand and supply as independent functions of price. Neither the aggregate quantity demanded nor the aggregate quantity supplied should be taken as an independent function of the price level. Figure 10.1 is rather to be interpreted as we have indicated, with movement along it showing how much the price level changes when real income changes for any reason. We have also shown the determinants of real income (total output) that cause it to change. To speak of changes in total output as responses to aggregate demand is not to employ the sort of aggregate curve we have just rejected. It is to say that changes in the basic determinants of real income alter the total quantity of spending, that is, buying, and thereby alter production. Aggregate demand refers here to a quantity, not to a curve that shows the usual demand relation to price and that is independent of supply.

THE BUSINESS CYCLE

What we want to know is, how much an increase in aggregate demand, however brought about, will raise the price level, and how much it will increase employment and real income. We have seen that we can generalize loosely to the effect that the output reaction will be relatively large when there is a lot of unemployment, and the price reaction will be relatively larger when there is little unemployment, with a "more nearly even" division in between the two extremes. But this is not very precise. Can we do better? The quantity theory did not result in any formulations that could give any more specific results correctly, though it is possible to adapt it to yield some state-

ments about the effects of changes in the money supply on the level of money income. The multiplier
analysis can likewise be broadened. It can then shed
some light on changes in real income even when prices
change, and can be adapted to show changes in money
income when only prices change if I increases. But
neither quantity nor multiplier analysis is able to show
precisely the amounts of both output and price
changes in instances when both do, in fact, change to
varying degrees. In short, both tools are useful to some
extent, but both leave us without an adequate answer
to the question of relative change of price and output.

Can a more empirical analysis give us the answer?
It might be thought that we could ascertain from available statistics the slope of our 10.1 curve for each
percentage of the labor force unemployed. Then indeed we could predict, knowing the percentage unemployed at any given time, how much price inflation
and how much increase in real income would result
from measures to stimulate the economy. But, alas, the
matter is not this simple either, though perhaps one
should not entirely disregard an estimate derived thus
from past experience. But the trouble is that situations
may and do differ substantially even though the percentage of unemployment may be the same. So, too,
the slope of the curve will differ from time to time.
The art of prediction—and it is an art and not just a
science—involves some guesswork and some luck,
though it can properly employ as much systematic
analysis and as much empirical data as is available. In-
formation on the technological factors mentioned may
indicate the extent of excess capacity and its distribu-

tion among critical sectors of the economy. When this is found to be different from that usually found at the comparable stage of the cycle, one's prediction would need to be altered accordingly. The art of predicting requires not only some knowledge of economics, but also an "ear to the ground." An ability to assess the likely business reactions to a situation is essential. And not least, the forecaster of price-output relations needs to be able to estimate the strength of labor unions in a given situation, the sorts of demands they will make, the amount of pressure they can put behind them, the amount of resistance they will meet, and the degrees to which each side will compromise under the likely pressures. No simple mathematical predictive formula will do when it is thus necessary to differentiate situations with similar percentages of unemployment.

Thus far we have been talking about movement to the right on the 10.1 curve. What about movement to the left? The fact is we do not move to the left on that curve; it is what may be called an irreversible curve. When aggregate demand declines, usually due to a fall in the rate of private real investment, the economy does not initially suffer rapid price deflation, and only then begin to develop unemployment and cut back production much. The downswing is much more likely to witness a drop in spending and sales, followed by a cutback in production that may become quite substantial before the general price level sags much. The price level has even been known to rise a little in the initial part of a downswing as maladjustments in the price structure at the peak of the boom are worked out and push up some prices that had not yet adjusted to higher costs. With the price-wage levels resistant as they are to downward pressure, the downswing of the cycle may not bring them the whole way back to the level of the preceding recession. The next upswing may therefore start from a higher base than the preceding upswing, thus imparting an inflationary trend to the price level. In view of this, the surprising thing is that the price level has been as stable as it has in the post-Korean War period.[1]

Because of the variation in the factors we have discussed, the relationship between real income and the price level has not been stable, though there is also, as we have seen, reason for expecting similarities in the pattern from time to time. A fuller exploration would require a more detailed study of business cycles and the monetary factors in the cycle.

INFLATION

We may bring our study to a conclusion by further consideration of inflation. A concern with the decline in the value of money has typically characterized the monetary theorist, and we live in a day when much is made of the decline in the value of the dollar. One thing should be quite clear—historically, the big inflations have been the result chiefly of war. War itself and the aftermath of war account for more inflation than any other single factor. Some notable inflations have come also from sharp increases, at certain times,

[1] For a good discussion of the degree of stability in the period, see Alvin Hansen, *Economic Issues of the 1960's* (New York: McGraw-Hill, 1960).

in the supplies of the monetary metals. But our analysis is concerned with more normal situations. We may recognize four types of inflation as we classify the major factors responsible for rising price levels: (1) Demand-pull inflation is the most common. As the name suggests, it is due to the total demand for goods rising faster than the total supply of goods. (2) Cost-push inflation is that attributable to upward pressure on the finished-goods price level deriving from rising costs of production. Most commonly the cost factor alleged to be responsible is rising money wage rates. This may be the factor if such wages rise faster than labor productivity rises. (3) Administered price inflation is that attributable to inflationary business pricing policies, where sufficient monopoly power exists to give effect to such policies. (4) Sectoral price inflation is the term that has been used when none of the above three categories properly characterizes the economy as a whole, but where one or another characterizes some important sector or sectors of the economy and the general price level is thereby affected.

Often the different factors work together, as in the wage-price spiral after World War II, so that it is virtually impossible to determine the precise amount of inflation properly attributable to one factor or another. When it comes to the control of inflation, however, the matter is a little clearer, for control of demand-pull inflation can be a crucial factor. If this is controlled, as by an appropriate monetary-fiscal policy, the most important contribution to the inflation problem will have been made. If the demand-pull factor is left uncontrolled, it may be impossible to exert much control over any other factors in an inflationary situation.

The form of the inflation problem that has become most prominent in recent years has to do with limiting the amount of inflation associated with efforts to maintain a high level of employment in the economy. There is general agreement on the goal of pushing the economy close to full employment, that is, toward the right-hand side of Figure 10.1, while minimizing inflation. It is not at all certain that we can have full employment, a stable price level, and the degree of economic freedom we now possess. There is yet no proof that we must give up one of the three either. Nor do we know how much of any one of the three we may have to give up to get a given proportion of the others. But what the trade-off may be in the future is not wholly a matter to be determined by the past, however much we may learn from the past. There are a number of issues involved in the inflation problem and its handling.[2] A crucial dilemma arises from the fact that it is in the interest of everybody to check inflation as we approach full employment, but some see an even bigger interest in doing things for themselves that are not compatible with minimizing inflation. They may succeed in such actions provided others do not try to do likewise. Some labor and business groups individually can gain by pushing up certain prices, provided all other such groups do not do likewise; for when all do likewise, all lose something by more inflation. It is difficult to ask any to forego possible gains for the

[2] For one of the best discussions of inflation, see G. L. Bach, *Inflation* (Providence, Rhode Island: Brown University Press, 1958).

sake of all, unless they have reasonable assurance that all will do likewise. But to compel all to "hold the line" and forego possible gains restricts present freedoms of labor and business. To request or to compel labor groups to "hold the line" while letting business groups price themselves into soaring profits is not a realistic policy either.

All this is the background for the famous "wage-price guidelines." These can be regarded as an essential supplement for a monetary-fiscal policy aimed at full employment with minimum inflation. There is no assurance that breaches in the guidelines will not be so numerous as to destroy them, but they may be the only way to enable us to avoid the unpleasant choice between high unemployment, substantial inflation at full employment, and direct government controls of prices and wages. The protection of the value of the dollar, while agreed to be important, is not the only concern. We have seen enough to understand that the actions of various groups, in the context of policies to promote general prosperity and stability, will do much to determine what trade-offs there will be, and what alternatives will be open to us, among employment, stable dollars, and specific freedoms.

Index

About the Author

Harlan M. Smith, Associate Professor of Economics at the University of Minnesota, received his Ph.D. degree from the University of Chicago. He began his professional career researching the applicability of inter-industry relations analysis for business cycle policy. He subsequently shifted his attention to monetary economics and various economic problems. He is the author of several articles on inflation and foreign trade policy as well as a study, published in 1962, entitled "Monetary Theory Resurveyed." He edited the report of a study on the local impact of foreign trade and a study guide for use with the American Economy television film course. He taught at Brown University from 1947 to 1950 and has been teaching at the University of Minnesota since 1950.